PREFACE.

The subject of "The Pelican Island" was suggested by a passage in Captain Flinders' Voyage to Terra Australis. Describing one of those numerous gulfs which indent the coast of New Holland, and are thickly spotted with small islands, he says : — " Upon two of these we found many young pelicans unable to fly. Flocks of the old birds were sitting upon the beaches of the lagoon, and it appeared that the islands were their breeding places ; not only so, but, from the number of skeletons and bones there scattered, it should seem that for ages these had been selected for the closing scene of their existence. Certainly, none more likely to be free from disturbance of every kind could have been chosen, than these islets of a hidden lagoon of an uninhabited island [called by Captain F. Kangaroo Island], situate upon an unknown coast, near the antipodes of Europe ; nor can any thing be more consonant to their feelings, if Pelicans have any, than quietly to resign their breath, surrounded by their progeny, and in the same spot where they first drew it." – Captain Flinders was particularly struck with the appearance of one of these islands, on the surface of which were scattered the relics of a great number of trees, prostrated by some tremendous storm, or, as he conjectured, self-ignited by the friction of dead branches in a strong wind. This fact (adopting the former hypothesis) suggested the catastrophe described at the close of the third Canto of the Poem.

Having determined not to encumber his volume with notes, which might plausibly have been done to a great extent, — and believing, that those readers, who shall be sufficiently interested in the poem to desire further knowledge of the subjects progressively reviewed in it, may readily satisfy themselves from popular books of voyages, and natural history, — the Author will merely offer, in this place, an illustration of the nature of coral reefs, extracted from Captain Basil Hall's Voyage to the Island of Loo Choo, in the Chinese Sea.

"The examination of a coral reef during the different stages of one tide, is particularly interesting. When the tide has left it for some time it becomes dry, and appears to be a compact rock, exceedingly hard and ragged ; but as the tide rises, and the waves begin to wash over it, the coral worms protrude themselves from holes which before were invisible. These animals are of a great variety of shapes and sizes, and in such prodigious numbers, that, in a short time, the whole surface of the rock appears to be alive and in motion. The most common worm is in the form of a star, with arms from four to six inches long, which are moved about with a rapid motion in all directions, probably to catch food. Others are so sluggish, that they may be mistaken for pieces of the rock, and are generally of a dark colour, and from four to five inches long, and two or three round. When the coral is broken about high-water mark, it is a solid hard stone ; but if any part of it be detached at a spot which the tide reaches every day, it is found to be full of worms of different lengths and colours, some being fine as a thread and several feet long, of a bright yellow, and sometimes of a blue colour ; others resemble snails, and some are not unlike lobsters in shape, but soft, and not above two inches long.

"The growth of coral appears to cease when the worm is no longer exposed to the washing of the sea. Thus a reef rises in the form of a cauliflower, till its top has gained the level of the highest tides, above which the worm has no power to advance, and the reef of course no longer extends itself upwards. The other parts in succession reach the surface, and there stop, forming in time a level field with steep sides all round. The reef, however, continually increases, and being prevented from growing higher, extends itself laterally in all directions. But the growth being as rapid at the upper edge as it is lower down, the steepness of the face of the reef is still preserved. These are the circumstances which render coral reefs so dangerous in navigation ; for, in the first place, they are seldom seen above the water ; and, in the next, their sides are so steep, that a ship's bow may strike against the rock before any change of soundings has given warning of the danger."

With these brief quotations to explain the two principal circumstances on which the poem is founded, the Author abandons his "Pelican Island" to the judgment of the public, having no hope to conciliate favour by apology or vindication, where he has painfully felt that both would be necessary, if the success or failure of his work did not wholly depend on the manner in which it has been executed. He only requests the reader to bear in mind, that the narrative is supposed to be delivered by the imaginary being who witnesses the series of events, *after* the whole has happened, and who therefore describes them in such language, and with such illustrations, as the knowledge which he *then* possessed enabled him to use, whether he be identified with the Author, or (if the latter will so far condescend) with the reader himself, as spectator, actor, thinker, in this masquerade of

"Truth severe by fairy-fiction drest."

Sheffield, July 19. 1827.

"It must be placed at the head of his works, whether we regard it as a whole, or in insulated passages . . ."
David Macbeth Moir

THE PELICAN ISLAND

WALMER POETRY

inaugural volume

Engraved by Joseph Brown

LONDON, ROUTLEDGE, WARNE & ROUTLEDGE, FARRINGDON STREET

THE PELICAN ISLAND

A Poem in Nine Cantos

by

James Montgomery

with a preface by the author
and seventeen illustrations by various hands

ADELAIDE
MICHAEL WALMER
2014

The Pelican Island first published 1827

Illustrations first published 1860 in *Poems of James Montgomery,*
edited by Robert Aris Willmott

This edition published 2014

by

Michael Walmer
49 Second Street
Gawler South
South Australia 5118

ISBN 978-0-9924220-6-6 paperback
ISBN 978-0-9924220-7-3 ebook

CONTENTS

— ❖ —

LIST OF ILLUSTRATIONS

ENGRAVED BY THE BROTHERS DALZIEL

— ═◦═◦═◦═══ —

THE

PELICAN ISLAND.

CANTO FIRST.

METHOUGHT I lived through ages, and beheld

Their generations pass so swiftly by me,

That years were moments in their flight, and hours

The scenes of crowded centuries reveal'd ;

While Time, Life, Death, the world's great actors, wrought

New and amazing changes : — these I sing.

Sky, sun, and sea were all the universe ;

The sky, one blue, interminable arch,

Without a breeze, a wing, a cloud ; the sun

Sole in the firmament, but in the deep,

Redoubled ; where the circle of the sea,

Invisible with calmness, seem'd to lie

Within the hollow of a lower heaven.

   I was a Spirit in the midst of these,

All eye, ear, thought ; existence was enjoyment ;

Light was an element of life, and air

The clothing of my incorporeal form, —

A form impalpable to mortal touch,

And volatile as fragrance from the flower,

Or music in the woodlands.   What the soul

Can make itself at pleasure, that I was ;

A child in feeling and imagination,

Learning new lessons still, as Nature wrought

Her wonders in my presence.   All I saw,

(Like Adam when he walk'd in Paradise,)

I knew and named by secret intuition.

Actor, spectator, sufferer, each in turn,

I ranged, explored, reflected. Now I sail'd,

And now I soar'd ; anon expanding, seem'd

Diffused into immensity, yet bound

Within a space too narrow for desire ;

The mind, the mind perpetual themes must task,

Perpetual power impel, and hope allure.

I and the silent sun were here alone,

But not companions ; high and bright he held

His course ; I gazed with admiration on him, —

There all communion ended ; and I sigh'd,

In loneliness unutterable sigh'd,

To feel myself a wanderer without aim,

An exile amid splendid desolation,

A prisoner with infinity surrounded.

The sun descended, dipp'd, and disappear'd ;

Then sky and sea were all the universe,

And I the only being in existence !

So thought I, and the thought, like ice and fire,

Went freezing, burning, withering, thrilling, through

    me.

Annihilation then had been deliverance,

While that eternity of solitude

Lay on my heart, hard struggling to break free,

As from a dream, when mountains press the sleeper.

    Darkness, meanwhile, disguised in twilight, crept

O'er air and ocean ; drearier gloom involved

My fainting senses, till a sudden ray

Of pensile lustre sparkled from the west ;

I flew to meet it, but drew never nearer,

While, vanishing and re-appearing oft,

At length it trembled out into a star.

My soul revived, and could I then have wept,

(Methought I did) with tears of fond delight,

How had I hail'd the gentle apparition,

As second life to me ; so sweetly welcome

The faintest semblance of society,

Though but a point to rest the eye upon,

To him who hath been utterly bereaved !

— Star after star, from some unseen abyss,

Came through the sky, like thoughts into the mind,

We know not whence ; till all the firmament

Was throng'd with constellations, and the sea

Strown with their images.   Amidst a sphere

Of twinkling lights, like living eyes, that look'd

At once on me from every side, I stood,

(Motion and rest with me were mere volition,)

Myself perhaps a star among the rest !

But here again I found no fellowship ;

Sight could not reach, nor keenest thought conceive

Their nature or their offices.   To me

They were but what they seem'd, and yet I felt

They must be more ; the mind hath no horizon,

It looks beyond the eye, and seeks for mind

In all it sees, or all it sees o'erruling.

Low in the east, ere long, the morning dawn

Shot upward, onward, and around the pole,

With arrowy glimpses traversing the shade.

Night's train, as they had kindled one by one,

Now one by one withdrew, reversing order,

Where those that came the latest, earliest went :

Day rose triumphant, and again to me

Sky, sun and sea were all the universe ;

But ah ! the glory had departed, and I long'd

For some untried vicissitude : — it came.

A breeze sprang up, and with caressing wing

Play'd like an unseen being on the water,

Slowly from slumber 'woke the unwilling main,

Curling and murmuring, till the infant waves

Leap'd on his lap, and laugh'd in air and sunshine :

Then all was bright and beautiful emotion,

And sweet accordance of susurrant sounds.

I felt the gay delirium of the scene ;

I felt the breeze and billow chase each other,

Like bounding pulses in my human veins :

For, though impassive to the elements,

The form I wore was exquisitely tuned

To Nature's sympathies ; joy, fear, hope, sorrow,

(As though I yet were in the body) moved,

Elated, shook, or tranquillized my soul.

Thus pass'd the day : night follow'd, deck'd with stars

Innumerable, and the pale new moon,

Beneath her feet, a slight inverted crescent,

Soon disappearing.

     Time flew on, and brought

Alternate morn and eve. The sun, the stars,

The moon through all her phases, waxing, waning,

The planets seeking rest, and finding none,

— These were the only objects in mine eye,

The constant burthen of my thoughts, perplex'd

With vain conjectures why they were created.

Once, at high noon, amidst a sultry calm,

Looking around for comfort, I descried,

Far on the green horizon's utmost verge,

A wreath of cloud ; to me a glad discovery,

For each new image sprang a new idea,

The germ of thoughts to come, that could not die,

The little vapour rapidly expanded,

Lowering and thickening till it hid the sun,

And threw a starless night upon the sea.

Eagerly, tremblingly, I watch'd the end.

Faint gleam'd the lightning, follow'd by no peal ;

Dreary and hollow moans foretold a gale ;

Nor long the issue tarried ; then the wind,

Unprison'd, blew its trumpet loud and shrill ;

Out flash'd the lightnings gloriously ; the rain

Came down like music, and the full-toned thunder

Roll'd in grand harmony throughout high heaven :

Till ocean, breaking from his black supineness,

Drown'd in his own stupendous uproar all

The voices of the storm beside ; meanwhile

A war of mountains raged upon his surface ;

Mountains each other swallowing, and again

New Alps and Andes, from unfathom'd valleys

Upstarting, join'd the battle ; like those sons

Of earth, — giants, rebounding as new-born

From every fall on their unwearied mother.

I glow'd with all the rapture of the strife :

Beneath was one wild whirl of foaming surges ;

Above the array of lightnings, like the swords

Of cherubim, wide brandish'd, to repel

Aggression from heaven's gates ; their flaming strokes

Quench'd momentarily in the vast abyss.

  The voice of Him who walks upon the wind,

And sets his throne upon the floods, rebuked

The headlong tempest in its mid-career,

And turn'd its horrors to magnificence.

The evening sun broke through the embattled

  clouds,

And threw round sky and sea, as by enchantment,

A radiant girdle, binding them to peace,

In the full rainbow's harmony of beams ;

No brilliant fragment, but one sevenfold circle,

That spann'd the horizon, meted out the heavens,

And underarch'd the ocean. 'Twas a scene,

That left itself for ever on my mind.

Night, silent, cool, transparent, crown'd the day ;

The sky receded further into space,

The stars came lower down to meet the eye,

Till the whole hemisphere, alive with light,

Twinkled from east to west by one consent.

The constellations round the arctic pole,

That never set to us, here scarcely rose,

But in their stead, Orion through the north

Pursued the Pleiads ; Sirius, with his keen,

Quick scintillations, in the zenith reign'd.

The south unveil'd its glories ; — there, the Wolf,

With eyes of lightning, watch'd the Centaur's spear ;

Through the clear hyaline, the Ship of Heaven

Came sailing from eternity ; the Dove,

On silver pinions, wing'd her peaceful way ;

There, at the footstool of Jehovah's throne,

The Altar, kindled from his presence, blazed ;

There, too, all else excelling, meekly shone

The Cross, the symbol of redeeming love :
The Heavens declared the glory of the Lord,
The firmament display'd his handy-work.

  With scarce inferior lustre gleam'd the sea,
Whose waves were spangled with phosphoric fire,
As though the lightnings there had spent their shafts,
And left the fragments glittering on the field.

  Next morn, in mockery of a storm, the breeze
And waters skirmish'd ; bubble-armies fought
Millions of battles on the crested surges,
And where they fell, all cover'd with their glory,
Traced in white foam on the cerulean main
Paths, like the milky-way among the stars.

  Charm'd with the spectacle, yet deeply touch'd

With a forlorn and not untender feeling —

"Why," said my thoughts within me, "why this waste

Of loveliness and grandeur unenjoy'd?

Is there no life throughout this fair existence?

Sky, sun, and sea, the moon, the stars, the clouds,

Wind, lightning, thunder, are but ministers ;

They know not what they are, nor what they do :

O for the beings for whom these were made !"

    Light as a flake of foam upon the wind,

Keel upward from the deep emerged a shell,

Shaped like the moon ere half her horn is fill'd ;

Fraught with young life, it righted as it rose,

And moved at will along the yielding water.

The native pilot of this little bark

Put out a tier of oars on either side,

Spread to the wafting breeze a two-fold sail,

And mounted up and glided down the billow

In happy freedom, pleased to feel the air

And wander in the luxury of light.

Worth all the dead creation, in that hour,

To me appear'd this lonely Nautilus,

My fellow-being, like myself *alive*.

Entranced in contemplation vague yet sweet,

I watch'd its vagrant course and rippling wake,

Till I forgot the sun amidst the heavens.

It closed, sunk, dwindled to a point, then nothing ;

While the last bubble crown'd the dimpling eddy,

Through which mine eye still giddily pursued it,

A joyous creature vaulted through the air, —

The aspiring fish that fain would be a bird,

On long light wings, that flung a diamond shower

Of dew-drops round its evanescent form,

Sprang into light, and instantly descended.

Ere I could greet the stranger as a friend,

Or mourn his quick departure, — on the surge

A shoal of Dolphins, tumbling in wild glee,

Glow'd with such orient tints, they might have been

The rainbow's offspring, when it met the ocean

In that resplendent vision I had seen.

While yet in ecstasy I hung o'er these,

With every motion pouring out fresh beauties,

As though the conscious colours came and went

At pleasure, glorying in their subtle changes, —

Enormous o'er the flood, Leviathan

Look'd forth, and from his roaring nostrils sent

Two fountains to the sky, then plunged amain

In headlong pastime through the closing gulf.

These were but preludes to the revelry

That reign'd at sunset : then the deep let loose

Its blithe adventurers to sport at large,

As kindly instinct taught them ; buoyant shells,

On stormless voyages, in fleets or single,

Wherried their tiny mariners ; aloof,

On wing-like fins, in bow-and-arrow figures,

The flying fishes darted to and fro ;

While spouting Whales projected wat'ry columns,

That turn'd to arches at their height, and seem'd

The skeletons of crystal palaces,

Built on the blue expanse, then perishing,

Frail as the element which they were made of :

Dolphins, in gambols, lent the lucid brine

Hues richer than the canopy of eve,

That overhung the scene with gorgeous clouds,

Decaying into gloom more beautiful

Than the sun's golden liveries which they lost :

Till light that hides, and darkness that reveals

The stars, — exchanging guard, like sentinels

Of day and night, — transform'd the face of nature :

Above was wakefulness, silence around,

Beneath, repose, — repose that reach'd even me.

Power, will, sensation, memory, fail'd in turn ;

My very essence seem'd to pass away,

Like a thin cloud that melts across the moon,

Lost in the blue immensity of heaven.

THE

PELICAN ISLAND.

CANTO SECOND.

LIFE'S intermitting pulse again went on :

I woke amidst the beauty of a morn,

That shone as bright within me as around.

The presence-chamber of the soul was full

Of flitting images and rapturous thoughts ;

For eye and mind were open'd to explore

The secrets of the abyss erewhile conceal'd.

The floor of ocean, never trod by man,

Was visible to me as heaven's round roof,

Which man hath never touch'd ; the multitude

Of living things, in that new hemisphere,

Gleam'd out of darkness, like the stars at midnight,

When moon nor clouds, with light or shade, obscure

    them.

For, as in hollows of the tide-worn reef,

Left at low water glistening in the sun,

Pellucid pools and rocks in miniature,

With their small fry of fishes, crusted shells,

Rich mosses, tree-like sea-weed, sparkling pebbles,

Enchant the eye, and tempt the eager hand

To violate the fairy paradise,

— So to my view the deep disclosed its wonders.

    In the free element beneath me swam,

Flounder'd, and dived, in play, in chase, in battle,

Fishes of every colour, form, and kind

(Strange forms, resplendent colours, kinds unnum-

    ber'd)

Which language cannot paint, and mariner

Hath never seen ; from dead Leviathan

To insect-millions peopling every wave ;

And nameless tribes, half-plant, half-animal,

Rooted and slumbering through a dream of life.

The livelier inmates to the surface sprang,

To taste the freshness of heaven's breath, and feel

That light is pleasant, and the sunbeam warm.

Most in the middle region sought their prey,

Safety, or pastime ; solitary some,

And some in pairs affectionately join'd ;

Others in shoals immense, like floating islands,

Led by mysterious instinct through that waste

And trackless region, though on every side

Assaulted by voracious enemies,

— Whales, sharks, and monsters, arm'd in front or

   jaw,

With swords, saws, spiral horns, or hooked fangs.

While ravening Death of slaughter ne'er grew weary,

Life multiplied the immortal meal as fast.

War, reckless, universal war, prevail'd ;

All were devourers, all in turn devour'd ;

Yet every unit in the uncounted sum

Of victims had its share of bliss, its pang,

And but a pang, of dissolution ; each

Was happy till its moment came, and then

Its first, last suffering, unforeseen, unfear'd,

Closed, with one struggle, pain and life for ever.

So He ordain'd, whose way is in the sea,

His path amidst great waters, and his steps

Unknown ; — whose judgments are a mighty deep,

Where plummet of Archangel's intellect

Could never yet find soundings, but from age

To age let down, drawn up, then thrown again,

With lengthen'd line and added weight, still fails ;

And still the cry in Heaven is "O the depth !"

    Thus, while bewilder'd with delight I gazed

On life in every shape it here assumed,

Congenial feeling made me follow it,

And try to be whatever I beheld :

By mental transmigration thus I pass'd

Through many a body, and in each assay'd

New instincts, powers, enjoyments, death itself ;

Till, weary with the fanciful pursuit,

I started from that idle reverie.

Then grew my heart more desolate than ever ;

Here had I found the beings which I sought,

— Beings for whom the universe was made,

Yet none of kindred with myself.   In vain

I strove to waken sympathy in breasts

Cold as the element in which they moved,

And inaccessible to fellowship

With me, as sun and stars, as winds and vapours :

Sense had they, but no more ; mind was not there.

They roam'd, they fed, they slept, they died, and left

Race after race, to roam, feed, sleep, then die,

And leave their like through endless generations ;

— Incessant change of actors, none of scene,

Through all that boundless theatre of strife !

Shrinking into myself again, I cried,

In bitter disappointment, — "Is this all ?"

I sent a glance at random from the cloud,

In which I then lay floating through mid-heaven,

To ocean's innermost recess ; — when, lo !

Another seal of nature's book was open'd,

Which held transported thought so deep entranced,

That Time, though borne through mightiest revo-
   lutions,

Seem'd, like the earth in motion, to stand still.

The works of ages grew beneath mine eye ;

As rapid intellect calls up events,

Combines, compresses, moulds them, with such power,

That, in a little page of memory,

An empire's annals lie, — a nation's fortunes

Pass in review, as motes through sunbeams pass,

Glistening and vanishing in quick succession,

Yet each distinct as though there were but one ;

— So thrice a thousand years, with all their issues,

Hurried before me, through a gleam of Time,

Between the clouds of two eternities, —

That whence they came, and that to which they
   tended.

Immeasurable continents beneath

The expanse of animated waters lay,

Not strown – as I have *since* discern'd the tracks

Of voyagers, — with shipwrecks and their spoils,

The wealth of merchants, the artillery

Of war, the chains of captives, and the gems,

That glow'd upon the brow of beauty ; crowns

Of monarchs, swords of heroes, anchors lost,

That never had let go their hold in storms ;

Helms, sunk in port, that steer'd adventurous barks

Round the wide world ; bones of dead men, that
made

A hidden Golgotha where they had fallen,

Unseen, unsepulchred, but not unwept

By lover, friend, relation, far away,

Long waiting their return to home and country,

And going down into their fathers' graves

With their grey hairs or youthful locks in sorrow,

To meet no more till seas give up their dead :

Some too – ay thousands – whom none living
   mourn'd,

None miss'd, — waifs in the universe, the last

Lorn links of kindred chains for ever sunder'd.

   Not such the spectacle I now survey'd :

No broken hearts lay there ; no aching heads,

For whose vast schemes the world was once too small,

And life too short, in Death's dark lap found rest

Beneath the unresting wave ; — but skeletons

Of Whales and Krakens here and there were scat-
   ter'd,

The prey when dead of tribes, their prey when living:

And, seen by glimpses, but awakening thoughts

Too sad for utterance, — relics huge and strange

Of the old world that perish'd by the flood,

Kept under chains of darkness till the judgment.

— Save these, lay ocean's bed, as from the hand

Of its Creator, hollow'd and prepared

For his unfathomable counsels there,

To work slow miracles of power divine,

From century to century, — nor less

Incomprehensible than heaven and earth

Form'd in six days by his commanding word.

With God a thousand years are as one day ;

He in one day can sum a thousand years :

All acts with Him are equal ; for no more

It costs Omnipotence to build a world,

And set a sun amidst the firmament,

Than mould a dew-drop, and light up its gem.

This was the landscape stretch'd beneath the flood:

— Rocks, branching out like chains of Alpine moun-
    tains ;

Gulfs intervening, sandy wildernesses,

Forests of growth enormous, caverns, shoals ;

Fountains upspringing, hot and cold, and fresh

And bitter, as on land ; volcanic fires

Fiercely out-flashing from earth's central heart,

Nor soon extinguish'd by the rush of waters

Down the rent crater to the unknown abyss

Of Nature's laboratory, where she hides

Her deeds from every eye except her Maker's :

— Such were the scenes which ocean open'd to me ;

Mysterious regions, the recluse abode

Of unapproachable inhabitants,

That dwelt in everlasting darkness there.

Unheard by them the roaring of the wind,

The elastic motion of the wave unfelt ;

Still life was theirs, well pleasing to themselves,

Nor yet unuseful, as my song shall show.

   Here, on a stony eminence, that stood,

Girt with inferior ridges, at the point,

Where light and darkness meet in spectral gloom,

Midway between the height and depth of ocean,

I mark'd a whirlpool in perpetual play,

As though the mountain were itself alive,

And catching prey on every side, with feelers

Countless as sunbeams, slight as gossamer :

Ere long transfigured, each fine film became

An independent creature, self-employ'd,

Yet but an agent in one common work,

The sum of all their individual labours.

Shapeless they seem'd, but endless shapes assumed ;

Elongated like worms, they writhed and shrunk

Their tortuous bodies to grotesque dimensions ;

Compress'd like wedges, radiated like stars,

Branching like sea-weed, whirl'd in dazzling rings ;

Subtle and variable as flickering flames,

Sight could not trace their evanescent changes,

Nor comprehend their motions, till minute

And curious observation caught the clew

To this live labyrinth, — where every one,

By instinct taught, perform'd its little task ;

— To build its dwelling and its sepulchre,

From its own essence exquisitely modell'd ;

There breed, and die, and leave a progeny,

Still multiplied beyond the reach of numbers,

To frame new cells and tombs ; then breed and die

As all their ancestors had done, — and rest,

Hermetically seal'd, each in its shrine,

A statue in this temple of oblivion !

Millions and millions thus, from age to age,

With simplest skill, and toil unwieariable,

No moment and no movement unimproved,

Laid line on line, on terrace terrace spread,

To swell the heightening, brightening gradual
    mound,

By marvellous structure climbing tow'rds the day.

Each wrought alone, yet all together wrought,

Unconscious, not unworthy, instruments,

By which a hand invisible was rearing

A new creation in the secret deep.

Omnipotence wrought in them, with them, by them ;

Hence what Omnipotence alone could do

Worms did.   I saw the living pile ascend,

The mausoleum of its architects,

Still dying upwards as their labours closed :

Slime the material, but the slime was turn'd

To adamant, by their petrific touch ;

Frail were their frames, ephemeral their lives,

Their masonry imperishable.   All

Life's needful functions, food, exertion, rest,

By nice economy of Providence

Were overruled to carry on the process,

Which out of water brought forth solid rock.

Atom by atom thus the burthen grew,

Even like the infant in the womb, till Time

Deliver'd ocean of that monstrous birth,

— A coral island, stretching east and west,

In God's own language to its parent saying,

" Thus far, nor farther, shalt thou go ; and here

Shall thy proud waves be stay'd :" – A point at first

It peer'd above those waves ; a point so small,

I just perceived it, fix'd where all was floating ;

And when a bubble cross'd it, the blue film

Expanded like a sky above the speck ;

That speck became a hand-breadth ; day and night

It spread, accumulated, and ere long

Presented to my view a dazzling plain,

White as the moon amid the sapphire sea ;

Bare at low water, and as still as death,

But when the tide came gurgling o'er the surface,

'Twas like a resurrection of the dead :

From graves innumerable, punctures fine

In the close coral, capillary swarms

Of reptiles, horrent as Medusa's snakes,

Cover'd the bald-pate reef ; then all was life,

And indefatigable industry ;

The artizans were twisting to and fro,

In idle-seeming convolutions ; yet

They never vanish'd with the ebbing surge,

Till pellicle on pellicle, and layer

On layer, was added to the growing mass.

Ere long the reef o'ertopt the spring-flood's height,

And mock'd the billows when they leapt upon it,

Unable to maintain their slippery hold,

And falling down in foam-wreaths round its verge.

Steep were the flanks, with precipices sharp,

Descending to their base in ocean-gloom.

Chasms few, and narrow, and irregular,

Form'd harbours, safe at once and perilous, —

Safe for defence, but perilous to enter.

A sea-lake shone amidst the fossil isle,

Reflecting in a ring its cliffs and caverns,

With heaven itself seen like a lake below.

Compared with this amazing edifice,

Raised by the weakest creatures in existence,

What are the works of intellectual man ?

Towers, temples, palaces, and sepulchres ;

Ideal images in sculptured forms,

Thoughts hewn in columns, or in domes expanded,

Fancies through every maze of beauty shown ;

Pride, gratitude, affection turn'd to marble,

In honour of the living or the dead ;

What are they ? – fine-wrought miniatures of art,

Too exquisite to bear the weight of dew,

Which every morn lets fall in pearls upon them,

Till all their pomp sinks down in mouldering relics,

Yet in their ruin lovelier than their prime !

— Dust in the balance, atoms in the gale,

Compared with these achievements in the deep,

Were all the monuments of olden time,

In days when there were giants on the earth :

— Babel's stupendous folly, though it aim'd

To scale heaven's battlements, was but a toy,

The plaything of the world in infancy : —

The ramparts, towers, and gates of Babylon,

Built for eternity, — though where they stood,

Ruin itself stands still for lack of work,

And Desolation keeps unbroken sabbath ; —

Great Babylon, in its full moon of empire,

Even when its "head of gold" was smitten off,

And from a monarch changed into a brute ; —

Great Babylon was like a wreath of sand,

Left by one tide, and cancell'd by the next : —

Egypt's dread wonders, still defying Time,

Where cities have been crumbled into sand,

Scatter'd by winds beyond the Libyan desert,

Or melted down into the mud of Nile,

And cast in tillage o'er the corn-sown fields,

Where Memphis flourish'd, and the Pharaohs reign'd:—

Egypt's grey piles of hieroglyphic grandeur,

That have survived the language which they speak,

Preserving its dead emblems to the eye,

Yet hiding from the mind what these reveal ;

— Her pyramids would be mere pinnacles,

Her giant statues, wrought from rocks of granite,

But puny ornaments for such a pile

As this stupendous mound of catacombs,

Fill'd with dry mummies of the builder-worms.

Thus far, with undiverted thought, and eye

Intensely fix'd on ocean's concave mirror,

I watch'd the process to its finishing stroke :

Then starting suddenly, as from a trance,

Once more to look upon the blessed sun,

And breathe the gladdening influence of the wind,

Darkness fell on me ; giddily my brain

Whirl'd like a torch of fire that seems a circle,

And soon to me the universe was nothing.

PELICAN ISLAND.

CANTO THIRD.

Nine times the age of man that coral reef

Had bleach'd beneath the torrid noon, and borne

The thunder of a thousand hurricanes,

Raised by the jealous ocean, to repel

That strange encroachment on his old domain.

His rage was impotent ; his wrath fulfill'd

The counsels of eternal Providence,

And 'stablish'd what he strove to overturn :

For every tempest threw fresh wrecks upon it ;

Sand from the shoals, exuviæ from the deep,

Fragments of shells, dead sloughs, sea-monsters'

   bones,

Whales stranded in the shallows, hideous weeds

Hurl'd out of darkness by the uprooting surges ;

These, with unutterable relics more,

Heap'd the rough surface, till the various mass,

By Nature's chemistry combined and purged,

Had buried the bare rock in crumbling mould,

Not unproductive, but from time to time

Impregnated with seeds of plants, and rife

With embryo animals, or torpid forms

Of reptiles, shrouded in the clefts of trees,

From distant lands, with branches, foliage, fruit,

Pluck'd up and wafted hither by the flood,

Death's spoils, and life's hid treasures, thus enrich'd

And colonized the soil ; no particle

Of meanest substance but in course was turn'd

To solid use or noble ornament.

All seasons were propitious ; every wind

From the hot Siroc to the wet Monsoon,

Temper'd the crude materials ; while heaven's dew

Fell on the sterile wilderness as sweetly

As though it were a garden of the Lord ;

Nor fell in vain ; each drop had its commission,

And did its duty, known to Him who sent it.

Such time had past, such changes had transfigured

The aspect of that solitary isle,

When I again in spirit, as before,

Assumed mute watch above it.   Slender blades

Of grass were shooting through the dark brown

    earth,

Like rays of light, transparent in the sun,

Or after showers with liquid gems illumined ;

Fountains through filtering sluices sallied forth,

And led fertility where'er they turn'd ;

Green herbage graced their banks, resplendent
  flowers
Unlock'd their treasures, and let flow their fragrance.
Then insect legions, prank'd with gaudiest hues,
Pearl, gold, and purple, swarm'd into existence ;
Minute and marvellous creations these !
Infinite multitudes on every leaf,
In every drop, by me discern'd at pleasure,
Were yet too fine for unenlighten'd eye,
— Like stars, whose beams have never reach'd our
  world,
Though science meets them midway in the heaven
With prying optics, weighs them in her scale,
Measures their orbs, and calculates their courses : —
Some barely visible, some proudly shone,
Like living jewels ; some grotesque, uncouth,
And hideous, — giants of a race of pigmies ;

These burrow'd in the ground, and fed on garbage,

Those lived deliciously on honey-dews,

And dwelt in palaces of blossom'd bells ;

Millions on millions, wing'd, and plumed in front,

And arm'd with stings for vengeance or assault,

Fill'd the dim atmosphere with hum and hurry ;

Children of light, and air, and fire they seem'd,

Their lives all ecstasy and quick cross motion.

    Thus throve this embryo universe, where all

That was to be was unbegun, or now

Beginning ; every day, hour, instant brought

Its novelty, though how or whence I knew not ;

Less than omniscience could not comprehend

The causes of effects that seem'd spontaneous,

And sprang in infinite succession, link'd

With kindred issues infinite as they,

For which almighty skill had laid the train

Even in the elements of chaos, — whence

The unravelling clew not for a moment lost

Hold of the silent hand that drew it out.

Thus He who makes and peoples worlds still works

In secrecy, behind a veil of light ;

Yet through that hiding of his power, such glimpses

Of glory break as strike presumption blind,

But humble and exalt the humbled soul,

Whose faith the things invisible discerns,

And God informing, guiding, ruling all : —

He speaks, 'tis done ; commands, and it stands fast,

He calls an island from the deep, — it comes ;

Ordains its culture, — soil and seed are there ;

Appoints inhabitants, — from climes unknown,

By undiscoverable paths, they flock

Thither ; — like passage-birds to us in spring ;

They were not yesterday, — and lo ! to-day

They are, — but what keen eye beheld them coming ?

    Here was the infancy of life, the age

Of gold in that green isle, itself new-born,

And all upon it in the prime of being,

Love, hope, and promise ; 'twas in miniature

A world unsoil'd by sin ; a Paradise

Where Death had not yet enter'd ; Bliss had newly

Alighted, and shut close his rainbow wings,

To rest at ease, nor dread intruding ill.

Plants of superior growth now sprang apace,

With moon-like blossoms crown'd, or starry glories ;

Light flexile shrubs among the greenwood play'd

Fantastic freaks, — they crept, they climb'd, they

    budded,

And hung their flowers and berries in the sun ;

As the breeze taught, they danced, they sung, they
   twined,
Their sprays in bowers, or spread the ground with
   net-work.
Through the slow lapse of undivided time,
Silently rising from their buried germs,
Trees lifted to the skies their stately heads,
Tufted with verdure, like depending plumage,
O'er stems unknotted, waving to the wind :
Of these in graceful form, and simple beauty,
The fruitful cocoa and the fragrant palm
Excell'd the wilding daughters of the wood,
That stretch'd unwieldy their enormous arms,
Clad with luxuriant foliage, from the trunk,
Like the old eagle, feather'd to the heel ;
While every fibre, from the lowest root
To the last leaf upon the topmost twig,

Was held by common sympathy, diffusing

Through all the complex frame unconscious life.

Such was the locust with its hydra boughs,

A hundred heads on one stupendous trunk ;

And such the mangrove, which, at full-moon flood,

Appear'd itself a wood upon the waters,

But when the tide left bare its upright roots,

A wood on piles suspended in the air ;

Such too the Indian fig, that built itself

Into a sylvan temple, arch'd aloof

With airy aisles and living colonnades,

Where nations might have worshipp'd God in peace.

From year to year their fruits ungather'd fell ;

Not lost, but quickening where they lay, they struck

Root downward, and brake forth on every hand,

Till the strong saplings, rank and file, stood up,

A mighty army, which o'erran the isle,

And changed the wilderness into a forest.

All this appear'd accomplish'd in the space
Between the morning and the evening star :
So, in his third day's work, Jehovah spake,
And Earth, an infant, naked as she came,
Out of the womb of chaos, straight put on
Her beautiful attire, and deck'd her robe
Of verdure with ten thousand glorious flowers,
Exhaling incense ; crown'd her mountain-heads
With cedars, train'd her vines around their girdles,
And pour'd spontaneous harvests at their feet.

Nor were those woods without inhabitants
Besides the ephemera of earth and air ;
— Where glid the sunbeams through the latticed
    boughs,

And fell like dew-drops on the spangled ground,

To light the diamond-beetle on his way ;

— Where cheerful openings let the sky look down

Into the very heart of solitude,

On little garden-plots of social flowers,

That crowded from the shades to peep at daylight ;

— Or where unpermeable foliage made

Midnight at noon, and chill, damp horror reign'd

O'er dead, fall'n leaves and slimy funguses ;

— Reptiles were quicken'd into various birth.

Loathsome, unsightly, swoln to obscene bulk,

Lurk'd the dark toad beneath the infected turf ;

The slow-worm crawl'd, the light cameleon climb'd,

And changed his colour as his place he changed ;

The nimble lizard ran from bough to bough,

Glancing through light, in shadow disappearing ;

The scorpion, many-eyed, with sting of fire,

Bred there, — the legion-fiend of creeping things ;

Terribly beautiful, the serpent lay,

Wreath'd like a coronet of gold and jewels,

Fit for a tyrant's brow ; anon he flew

Straight as an arrow shot from his own rings,

And struck his victim, shrieking ere it went

Down his strain'd throat, that open sepulchre.

Amphibious monsters haunted the lagoon ;

The hippopotamus, amidst the flood,

Flexile and active as the smallest swimmer ;

But on the bank, ill balanced and infirm,

He grazed the herbage, with huge head declined,

Or lean'd to rest against some ancient tree.

The crocodile, the dragon of the waters,

In iron panoply, fell as the plague,

And merciless as famine, cranch'd his prey,

While from his jaws, with dreadful fangs all serried,

The life-blood dyed the waves with deadly streams.

The seal and the sea-lion, from the gulf,

Came forth, and couching with their little ones,

Slept on the shelving rocks that girt the shore,

Securing prompt retreat from sudden danger :

The pregnant turtle, stealing out at eve,

With anxious eye, and trembling heart, explored

The loneliest coves, and in the loose warm sand

Deposited her eggs, which the sun hatch'd :

Hence the young brood, that never knew a parent,

Unburrow'd and by instinct sought the sea ;

Nature herself, with her own gentle hand,

Dropping them one by one into the flood,

And laughing to behold their antic joy,

When launch'd in their maternal element.

The vision of that brooding world went on ;

Millions of beings yet more admirable

Than all that went before them now appear'd ;

Flocking from every point of heaven, and filling

Eye, ear, and mind with objects, sounds, emotions

Akin to livelier sympathy and love

Than reptiles, fishes, insects, could inspire

— Birds, the free tenants of land, air, and ocean,

Their forms all symmetry, their motions grace ;

In plumage, delicate and beautiful,

Thick without burthen, close as fishes' scales,

Or loose as full-blown poppies to the breeze ;

With wings that might have had a soul within them,

They bore their owners by such sweet enchantment ;

— Birds, small and great, of endless shapes and
   colours,

Here flew and perch'd, there swam and dived at pleasure;

Watchful and agile, uttering voices wild

And harsh, yet in accordance with the waves

Upon the beach, the winds in caverns moaning,

Or winds and waves abroad upon the water.

Some sought their food among the finny shoals,

Swift darting from the clouds, emerging soon

With slender captives glittering in their beaks ;

These in recesses of steep crags constructed

Their eyries inaccessible, and train'd

Their hardy broods to forage in all weathers :

Others, more gorgeously apparell'd, dwelt

Among the woods, on Nature's dainties feeding,

Herbs, seeds, and roots ; or, ever on the wing,

Pursuing insects through the boundless air :

In hollow trees or thickets these conceal'd

Their exquisitely woven nests ; where lay

Their callow offspring, quiet as the down

On their own breasts, till from her search the dam

With laden bill return'd, and shared the meal

Among her clamorous supplicants, all agape ;

Then, cowering o'er them with expanded wings,

She felt how sweet it is to be a mother.

Of these, a few, with melody untaught,

Turn'd all the air to music within hearing,

Themselves unseen ; while bolder quiristers

On loftiest branches strain'd their clarion-pipes,

And made the forest echo to their screams

Discordant, — yet there was no discord there,

But temper'd harmony ; all tones combining,

In the rich confluence of ten thousand tongues,

To tell of joy and to inspire it. Who

Could hear such concert, and not join in chorus ?

Not I ; — sometimes entranced, I seem'd to float

Upon a buoyant sea of sounds : again

With curious ear I tried to disentangle

The maze of voices, and with eye as nice

To single out each minstrel, and pursue

His little song through all its labyrinth,

Till my soul enter'd into him, and felt

Every vibration of his thrilling throat,

Pulse of his heart, and flutter of his pinions.

Often, as one among the multitude,

I sang from very fullness of delight ;

Now like a winged fisher of the sea,

Now a recluse among the woods, — enjoying

The bliss of all at once, or each in turn.

In storm and calm, through every change of season,

Long flourish'd thus that era of our isle ;

It could not last for ever : mark the end.

A cloud arose amid the tranquil heaven,

Like a man's hand, but held a hurricane

Within its grasp.   Compress'd into a point,

The tempest struggled to break loose.   No breath

Was stirring, yet the billows roll'd aloof,

And the air moan'd portentously ; ere long

The sky was hidden, darkness to be felt

Confounded all things ; land and water vanish'd,

And there was silence through the universe ;

Silence, that made my soul as desolate

As the blind solitude around.   Methought

That I had pass'd the bitterness of death

Without the agony, — had, unaware,

Enter'd the unseen world, and in the gap

Between the life that is and that to come,

Awaited judgment.   Fear and trembling seized

All that was mortal or immortal in me :

A moment, and the gates of Paradise

Might open to receive, or Hell be moved

To meet me.   Strength and spirit fail'd ;

Eternity enclosed me, and I knew not,

Knew not, even then, my destiny.   To doubt

Was to despair ; — I doubted and despair'd.

Then horrible delirium whirl'd me down

To ocean's nethermost recess ; the waves

Disparting freely, let me fall, and fall,

Lower and lower, passive as a stone,

Yet rack'd with miserable pangs, that gave

The sense of vain but violent resistance :

And still the depths grew deeper ; still the ground

Receded from my feet as I approach'd it.

O how I long'd to light on rocks, that sunk

Like quicksands ere I touch'd them ; or to hide

In caverns ever open to ingulf me,

But, like the horizon's limit, never nearer !

Meanwhile the irrepressible tornado

Burst, and involved the elements in chaos ;

Wind, rain, and lightning, in one vast explosion,

Rush'd from the firmament upon the deep.

Heaven's adamantine arch seem'd rent asunder,

And following in a cataract of ruins

My swift descent through bottomless abysses,

Where ocean's bed had been absorb'd in nothing.

I know no farther.   When again I saw

The sun, the sea, the island, all was calm,

And all was desolation : not a tree,

Of thousands flourishing erewhile so fair,

But now was split, uprooted, snapt in twain,

Or hurl'd with all its honours to the dust.

Heaps upon heaps, the forest giants lay,

Even like the slain in battle, fall'n to rise

No more, till heaven, and earth, and sea, with all

Therein, shall perish, as to me they seem'd

To perish in that ruthless hurricane.

THE

PELICAN ISLAND.

CANTO FOURTH.

NATURE and Time were twins.   Companions still,

Their unretarded, unreturning flight

They hold together.   Time, with one sole aim,

Looks ever onward, like the moon through space,

With beaming forehead, dark and bald behind,

Nor ever lost a moment in his course.

Nature looks all around her, like the sun,

And keeps her works, like his dependent worlds,

In constant motion.   She hath never miss'd

One step in her victorious march of change,

For chance she knows not ; He who made her, gave

His daughter power o'er all except Himself,

— Power in whate'er she does to do *his* will :

Behold the true, the royal law of Nature ! –

Hence failures, hinderances, and devastations

Are turn'd to trophies of exhaustless skill,

That out of ruin brings forth strength and beauty,

Yea life and immortality from death.

    I gazed in consternation on the wreck

Of that fair island, strown with prostrate trees,

The soil plough'd up with horrid inundations,

The surface black with sea-weed, not a glimpse

Of verdure peeping ; stems, boughs, foliage lay

Rent, broken, clotted, perishing in slime.

" How are the mighty fallen !" I exclaim'd ;

" Surely the feller hath come up among ye,

And with a stroke invisible hewn down

The growth of centuries in one dark hour !

Is this the end of all perfection ?   This

The abortive issue of a new creation,

Erewhile so fruitful in abounding joys,

And hopes fulfilling more than all they promised ?

Ages to come can but repair this ravage ;

The past is lost for ever.   Reckless Time

Stays not ; astonied Nature stands aghast,

And wrings her hands in silent agony,

Amidst the annihilation of her works. ”

Thus raved I ; but I wrong'd thee, glorious Nature !

With whom adversity is but transition.

Thou never didst despair, wert never foil'd,

Nor weary with exhaustion, since the day,

When, at the word “ Let there be light, ” light sprang

And show'd thee rising from primeval darkness,

That fell back like a veil from thy young form,

And Chaos fled before the apparition.

    While yet mine eye was mourning o'er the scene,

Nature and Time were working miracles :

The isle was renovated ; grass and flowers

Crept quietly around the fallen trees ;

A deeper soil embedded them, and o'er

The common sepulchre of all their race

Threw a rich covering of embroider'd turf,

Lovely to look on as the tranquil main,

When, in his noonward track, the unclouded sun

Tints the green waves with every hue of heaven,

More exquisitely brilliant and aerial

Than morn or evening's gaudier pageantry.

Amidst that burial of the mighty dead,

There was a resurrection from the dust

Of lowly plants, impatient for the light,

Long interrupted by o'ershadowing woods,

While in the womb of earth their embryos tarried,

Unfructifying, yet imperishable.

Huge remnants of the forest stood apart,

Like Tadmor's pillars in the wilderness,

Startling the traveller 'midst his thoughts of home ;

— Bare trunks of broken trees, that gave their heads

To the wind's axe, but would not yield their roots

To the uptearing violence of the floods.

From these a slender race of scions sprang,

Which with their filial arms embraced and shelter'd

The monumental relics of their sires ;

But, limited in number, scatter'd wide,

And slow of growth, they overran no more

The Sun's dominions in that open isle.

Meanwhile the sea-fowl, that survived the storm,

Whose rage had fleck'd the waves with shatter'd

   plumes

And weltering carcasses, the prey of sharks,

Came from their fastnesses among the rocks,

And multiplied like clouds when rains are brooding,

Or flowers, when clear warm sunshine follows rain.

The inland birds had perish'd, nor again,

By airy voyagers from shores unknown,

Was silence broken on the unwooded plains :

Another race of wing'd inhabitants

Erelong possess'd and peopled all the soil.

   The sun had sunk where sky and ocean meet,

And each might seem the other ; sky below,

With richest garniture of clouds inlaid ;

Ocean above with isles and continents,

Illumined from a source no longer seen :

Far in the east, through heaven's intenser blue,

Two brilliant sparks, like sudden stars, appear'd ;

Not stars indeed, but birds of mighty wing,

Retorted neck, and javelin-pointed bill,

That made the air sigh as they cut it through.

They gain'd upon the eye, and as they came,

Enlarged, grew brighter, and display'd their forms

Amidst the golden evening ; pearly white,

But ruby-tinctured.   On the loftiest cliff

They settled, hovering ere they touch'd the ground,

And uttering, in a language of their own,

Yet such as every ear might understand,

And every bosom answer, notes of joy,

And gratulation for that resting-place.

Stately and beautiful they stood, and clapt

Their van-broad pinions, streak'd their ruffled plumes,

And ever and anon broke off to gaze,

With yearning pleasure, told in gentle murmurs,

On that strange land their destined home and

    country.

Night round them threw her brown transparent

    gloom,

Through which their lonely images yet shone,

Like things unearthly, while they bow'd their heads

On their full bosoms, and reposed till morn.

I knew the Pelicans, and cried – " All hail !

Ye future dwellers in the wilderness !"

    At early dawn I mark'd them in the sky,

Catching the morning colours on their plumes ;

Not in voluptuous pastime revelling there,

Among the rosy clouds, while orient heaven

Flamed like the opening gates of Paradise,

Whence issued forth the Angel of the sun,

And gladden'd Nature with returning day :

— Eager for food their searching eyes they fix'd

On ocean's unroll'd volume, from an height,

That brought immensity within their scope ;

Yet with such power of vision look'd they down,

As though they watch'd the shell-fish slowly gliding

O'er sunken rocks, or climbing trees of coral.

On indefatigable wing upheld,

Breath, pulse, existence, seem'd suspended in them ;

They were as pictures painted on the sky ;

Till suddenly, aslant, away they shot,

Like meteors changed from stars to gleams of light-
    ning,

And struck upon the deep ; where, in wild play,

Their quarry flounder'd, unsuspecting harm,

With terrible voracity, they plunged

Their heads among the affrighted shoals, and beat

A tempest on the surges with their wings,

Till flashing clouds of foam and spray conceal'd them.

Nimbly they seized and secreted their prey,

Alive and wriggling in the elastic net,

Which Nature hung beneath their grasping beaks ;

Till, swoln with captures, the unwieldy burthen

Clogg'd their slow flight, as heavily to land

These mighty hunters of the deep return'd.

There on the cragged cliffs they perch'd at ease,

Gorging their hapless victims one by one ;

Then full and weary, side by side, they slept,

Till evening roused them to the chase again.

Harsh seems the ordinance, that life by life

Should be sustain'd, and yet when all must die,

And be like water spilt upon the ground,

Which none can gather up, — the speediest fate,

Though violent and terrible, is best.

O with what horrors would creation groan, —

What agonies would ever be before us,

Famine and pestilence, disease, despair,

Anguish and pain in every hideous shape,

Had all to wait the slow decay of Nature !

Life were a martyrdom of sympathy ;

Death, lingering, raging, writhing, shrieking torture ;

The grave would be abolish'd ; this gay world

A valley of dry bones, a Golgotha,

In which the living stumbled o'er the dead,

Till they could fall no more, and blind perdition

Swept frail mortality away for ever.

'Twas wisdom, mercy, goodness, that ordain'd

Life in such infinite profusion, — Death

So sure, so prompt, so multiform to those

That never sinn'd, that know not guilt, that fear

No wrath to come, and have no heaven to lose.

Love found that lonely couple on their isle,

And soon surrounded them with blithe companions.

The noble birds, with skill spontaneous, framed

A nest of reeds among the giant-grass,

That waved in lights and shadows o'er the soil.

There, in sweet thraldom, yet unweening why,

The patient dam, who ne'er till now had known

Parental instinct, brooded o'er her eggs,

Long ere she found the curious secret out,

That life was hatching in their brittle shells.

Then, from a wild rapacious bird of prey,

Tamed by the kindly process, she became

That gentlest of all living things — a mother ;

Gentlest while yearning o'er her naked young,

Fiercest when stirr'd by anger to defend them.

Her mate himself the softening power confess'd,

Forgot his sloth, restrain'd his appetite,

And ranged the sky and fish'd the stream for her.

Or, when o'erwearied Nature forced her off

To shake her torpid feathers in the breeze,

And bathe her bosom in the cooling flood,

He took her place, and felt through every nerve,

While the plump nestlings throbb'd against his heart,

The tenderness that makes the vulture mild ;

Yea, half unwillingly his post resign'd,

When, home-sick with the absence of an hour,

She hurried back, and drove him from her seat

With pecking bill, and cry of fond distress,

Answer'd by him with murmurs of delight,

Whose gutturals harsh to her were love's own music.

Then, settling down, like foam upon the wave,

White, flickering, effervescent, soon subsiding,

Her ruffled pinions smoothly she composed ;

And, while beneath the comfort of her wings,

Her crowded progeny quite fill'd the nest,

The halcyon sleeps not sounder, when the wind

Is breathless, and the sea without a curl,

— Nor dreams the halcyon of serener days,

Or nights more beautiful with silent stars,

Than, in that hour, the mother Pelican,

When the warm tumults of affection sunk

Into calm sleep, and dreams of what they were,

— Dreams more delicious than reality.

— He sentinel beside her stood, and watch'd,

With jealous eye, the raven in the clouds,

And the rank sea-mews wheeling round the cliffs.

Woe to the reptile then that ventured nigh ;

The snap of his tremendous bill was like

Death's scythe, down-cutting every thing it struck.

The heedless lizard, in his gambols, peep'd

Upon the guarded nest, from out the flowers,

But paid the instant forfeit of his life ;

Nor could the serpent's subtlety elude

Capture, when gliding by, nor in defence

Might his malignant fangs and venom save him.

Erelong the thriving brood outgrew their cradle,

Ran through the grass, and dabbled in the pools ;

No sooner denizens of earth than made

Free both of air and water ; day by day,

New lessons, exercises, and amusements

Employ'd the old to teach, the young to learn.

Now floating on the blue lagoon behold them ;

The Sire and Dam in swanlike beauty steering,

Their Cygnets following through the foamy wake,

Picking the leaves of plants, pursuing insects,

Or catching at the bubbles as they broke :

Till on some minor fry, in reedy shallows,

With flapping pinions and unsparing beaks,

The well-taught scholars plied their double art,

To fish in troubled waters, and secure

The petty captives in their maiden pouches ;

Then hurry with their banquet to the shore,

With feet, wings, breast, half-swimming and half-

    flying.

But when their pens grew strong to fight the storm,

And buffet with the breakers on the reef,

The Parents put them to severer proof :

On beetling rocks the little ones were marshall'd ;

There, by endearments, stripes, example urged

To try the void convexity of heaven,

And plough the ocean's horizontal field.

Timorous at first they flutter'd round the verge,

Balanced and furl'd their hesitating wings,

Then put them forth again with steadier aim ;

Now, gaining courage as they felt the wind

Dilate their feathers, fill their airy frames

With buoyancy that bore them from their feet,

They yielded all their burthen to the breeze,

And sail'd and soar'd where'er their guardians led ;

Ascending, hovering, wheeling, or alighting,

They search'd the deep in quest of nobler game

Than yet their inexperience had encounter'd ;

With these they battled in that element,

Where wings or fins were equally at home,

Till, conquerors in many a desperate strife,

They dragg'd their spoils to land, and gorged at

    leisure.

    Thus perfected in all the arts of life,

That simple Pelicans require, — save one,

Which mother-bird did never teach her daughter,

— The inimitable art to build a nest ;

Love, for his own delightful school, reserving

That mystery which novice never fail'd

To learn infallibly when taught by him :

— Hence that small masterpiece of Nature's art,

Still unimpair'd, still unimproved, remains

The same in site, material, shape, and texture.

While every kind a different structure frames,

All build alike of each peculiar kind :

The nightingale, that dwelt in Adam's bower,

And pour'd her stream of music through his dreams ;

The soaring lark, that led the eye of Eve

Into the clouds, her thoughts into the heaven

Of heavens, where lark nor eye can penetrate ;

The dove, that perch'd upon the Tree of Life,

And made her bed among its thickest leaves ;

All the wing'd habitants of Paradise,

Whose songs once mingled with the songs of Angels,

Wove their first nests as curiously and well

As the wood-minstrels in our evil day,

After the labours of six thousand years,

In which their ancestors have fail'd to add,

To alter or diminish, any thing

In that, of which Love only knows the secret,

And teaches every mother for herself,

Without the power to impart it to her offspring :

— Thus perfected in all the arts of life,

That simple Pelicans require, save this,

Those Parents drove their young away ; the young

Gaily forsook their parents.   Soon enthrall'd

With love-alliances among themselves,

They built their nests, as happy instinct wrought

Within their bosoms, wakening powers unknown,

Till sweet necessity was laid upon them ;

They bred, and rear'd their little families,

As they were train'd and disciplined before.

Thus wings were multiplied from year to year,

And ere the patriarch-twain, in good old age,

Resign'd their breath beside that ancient nest,

In which themselves had nursed a hundred broods,

The isle was peopled with their progeny.

THE

PELICAN ISLAND.

CANTO FIFTH.

MEANWHILE, not idle, though unwatch'd by me,

The coral-architects in silence rear'd

Tower after tower beneath the dark abyss,

Pyramidal in form the fabrics rose,

From ample basements narrowing to the height,

Until they pierced the surface of the flood,

And dimpling eddies sparkled round their peaks.

Then (if great things with small may be compared)

They spread like water-lilies, whose broad leaves

Make green and sunny islets on the pool,

For golden flies, on summer-days, to haunt,

Safe from the lightning-seizure of the trout ;

Or yield their laps to catch the minnow, springing

Clear from the stream to 'scape the ruffian pike,

That prowls in disappointed rage beneath,

And wonders where the little wretch found refuge.

One headland topt the waves, another follow'd ;

A third, a tenth, a twentieth soon appear'd,

Till the long-barren gulf in travail lay

With many an infant struggling into birth.

Larger they grew and lovelier, when they breathed

The vital air, and felt the genial sun ;

As though a living spirit dwelt in each,

Which, like the inmate of a flexile shell,

Moulded the shapeless slough with its own motion,

And painted it with colours of the morn.

Amidst that group of younger sisters, stood

The Isle of Pelicans, as stands the moon

At midnight, queen among the minor stars,

Differing in splendour, magnitude, and distance.

So look'd that archipelago ; small isles,

By interwinding channels link'd yet sunder'd ;

All flourishing in peaceful fellowship,

Like forest oaks that love society :

— Of various growth and progress ; here, a rock

On which a single palm-tree waved its banner ;

There, sterile tracts unmoulder'd into soil ;

Yonder, dark woods whose foliage swept the water,

Without a speck of turf, or line of shore,

As though their roots were anchor'd in the ocean.

But most were gardens redolent with flowers,

And orchards bending with Hesperian fruit,

That realized the dreams of olden time.

Throughout this commonwealth of sea-sprung lands,

Life kindled in ten thousand happy forms,

Earth, air, and ocean were all full of life.

Still highest in the rank of being, soar'd

The fowls amphibious, and the inland tribes

Of dainty plumage or melodious song.

In gaudy robes of many-colour'd patches,

The parrots swung like blossoms on the trees,

While their harsh voices undeceived the ear.

More delicately pencill'd, finer drawn

In shape and lineament ; too exquisite

For gross delights ; the Birds of Paradise

Floated aloof, as though they lived on air,

And were the orient progeny of heaven,

Or spirits made perfect veil'd in shining raiment,

From flower to flower, where wild bees flew and sung,

As countless, small, and musical as they,

Showers of bright humming-birds came down, and

    plied

The same ambrosial task, with slender bill

Extracting honey, hidden in those bells,

Whose richest blooms grew pale beneath the blaze

Of twinkling winglets hovering o'er their petals,

Brilliant as raindrops, when the western sun

Sees his own miniature of beams in each.

High on the cliffs, down on the shelly reef,

Or gliding like a silver-shaded cloud

Through the blue heaven, the mighty albatross

Inhaled the breezes, sought his humble food,

Or, where his kindred like a flock reposed,

Without a shepherd, on the grassy downs,

Smooth'd his white fleece, and slumber'd in their midst.

Wading through marshes, where the rank sea-weed

With spongy moss and flaccid lichens strove,

Flamingos, in their crimson tunics, stalk'd

On stately legs, with far-exploring eye ;

Or fed and slept, in regimental lines,

Watch'd by their sentinels, whose clarion-screams

All in an instant woke the startled troop,

That mounted like a glorious exhalation,

And vanish'd through the welkin far away,

Nor paused till, on some lonely coast alighting,

Again their gorgeous cohort took the field.

   The fierce sea-eagle, humble in attire,

In port terrific, from his lonely eyrie,

(Itself a burthen for the tallest tree)

Look'd down o'er land and sea as his dominions :

Now, from long chase, descending with his prey,

Young seal or dolphin, in his deadly clutch,

He fed his eaglets in the noon-day sun :

Nor less at midnight ranged the deep for game ;

At length entrapp'd with his own talons, struck

Too deep to be withdrawn, where a strong shark,

Roused by the anguish, with impetuous plunge,

Dragg'd his assailant down into the abyss,

Struggling in vain for liberty and life ;

His young ones heard their parent's dying shrieks,

And watch'd in vain for his returning wing.

Here ran the stormy petrels on the waves,

As though they were the shadows of themselves

Reflected from a loftier flight through space.

The stern and gloomy raven haunted here,

A hermit of the atmosphere, on land

Among vociferating crowds a stranger,

Whose hoarse, low, ominous croak disclaim'd com-

    munion

With those, upon the offal of whose meals

He gorged alone, or tore their own rank corses.

The heavy penguin, neither fish nor fowl,

With scaly feathers and with finny wings,

Plump'd stone-like from the rock into the gulf,

Rebounding upward swift as from a sling.

Through yielding water as through limpid air,

The cormorant, Death's living arrow, flew,

Nor ever miss'd a stroke, or dealt a second,

So true the infallible destroyer's aim.

    Millions of creatures such as these, and kinds

Unnamed by man, possess'd those busy isles ;

Each, in its brief existence, to itself,

The first, last being in the universe,

With whom the whole began, endured, and ended :

Blest ignorance of bliss, not made for them !

Happy exemption from the fear of death,

And that which makes the pangs of death immortal,

The undying worm, the fire unquenchable,

— Conscience, the bosom-hell of guilty man !

The eyes of all look'd up to Him, whose hand

Had made them, and supplied their daily need ;

Although they knew Him not, they look'd to Him ;

And He, whose mercy is o'er all his works,

Forgot not one of his large family,

But cared for each as for an only child.

They plough'd not, sow'd not, gather'd not in barns,

Thought not of yesterday, nor knew to-morrow ;

Yet harvests inexhaustible they reap'd

In the prolific furrows of the main ;

Or from its sunless caverns brought to light

Treasures for which contending kings might war, —

Gems, for which queens would yield their hands to

    slaves, —

By them despised as valueless and nought ;

From the rough shell they pick'd the luscious food,

And left a prince's ransom in the pearl.

    Nature's prime favourites were the Pelicans ;

High-fed, long-lived, and sociable and free,

They ranged in wedded pairs, or martial bands,

For play or slaughter. Oft have I beheld

A little army take the wat'ry field,

With outstretched pinions form a spacious ring,

Then pressing to the centre, through the waves,

Enclose thick shoals within their narrowing toils,

Till multitudes entangled fell a prey :

Or, when the flying-fish, in sudden clouds,

Burst from the sea, and flutter'd through the air,

These giant-fowlers snapt them like musquitos

By swallows hunted through the summer sky.

I turn'd again to look upon that isle,

Whence from one pair those colonies had issued

That through these Cyclades at freedom roved,

Fish'd every stream, and fed on every shore ;

When, lo ! a spectacle of strange extremes

Awaken'd sweet and melancholy thoughts :

All that is helpless, beautiful, endearing

In infancy, in prime of youth, in love ;

All that is mournful in decay, old age,

And dissolution ; all that awes the eye,

And chills the bosom, in the sad remains

Of poor mortality, which last awhile,

To shew that life hath been, but is no longer ;

— All these in blended images appear'd,

Exulting, brooding, perishing before me.

It was a land of births. — Unnumber'd nests,

Of reeds and rushes, studded all the ground.

A few were desolate and fallen to ruin ;

Many were building from those waste materials ;

On some the dams were sitting, till the stroke

Of their quick bills should break the prison-shells,

And let the little captives forth to light,

With their first breath demanding food and shelter.

In others I beheld the brood new-fledged,

Struggling to clamber out, take wing and fly

Up to the heavens, or fathom the abyss.

Meanwhile the parent from the sea supplied

A daily feast, and from the pure lagoon

Brought living water in her sack, to cool

The impatient fever of their clamorous throats.

No need had she, as hieroglyphics feign,

(A mystic lesson of maternal love)

To pierce her breast, and with the vital stream,

Warm from its fountain, slake their thirst in blood,

— The blood which nourish'd them ere they were

    hatch'd,

While the crude egg within herself was forming.

    It was a land of death. — Between those nests,

The quiet earth was feather'd with the spoils

Of aged Pelicans, that hither came

To die in peace, where they had spent in love

The sweetest periods of their long existence.

Where they were wont to build, and breed their

    young,

There they lay down to rise no more for ever,

And close their eyes upon the dearest sight

On which their living eyes had loved to dwell,

— The nest where every joy to them was centred.

There rife corruption tainted them so lightly,

The moisture seem'd to vanish from their relics,

As dew from gossamer, that leaves the net-work

Spread on the ground, and glistening in the sun ;

Thus when a breeze the ruffled plumage stirr'd,

That lay like drifted snow upon the soil,

Their slender skeletons were seen beneath,

So delicately framed, and half transparent,

That I have marvell'd how a bird so noble,

When in his full magnificent attire,

With pinions wider than the king of vultures',

And down elastic, thicker than the swan's,

Should leave so small a cage of ribs to mark

Where vigorous life had dwelt a hundred years.

    Such was that scene ; the dying and the dead,

Next neighbours to the living and the unborn.

O how much happiness was here enjoy'd !

How little misery had been suffer'd here !

Those humble Pelicans had each fulfill'd

The utmost purpose of its span of being,

And done its duty in its narrow circle,

As surely as the sun, in his career,

Accomplishes the glorious end of his.

THE

PELICAN ISLAND.

CANTO SIXTH.

" And thus, " methought, " ten thousand suns may
   lead

The stars to glory in their annual courses ;

Moons without number thus may wax and wane,

And winds alternate blow in cross-monsoons,

While here – through self-beginning rounds, self-
   ending,

Then self-renew'd, without advance or failure, —

Existence fluctuates only like the tide,

Whose everlasting changes bring no change,

But billow follows billow to the shore,

Recoils, and billow out of billow swells ;

An endless whirl of ebbing, flowing foam,

Where every bubble is like every other,

And ocean's face immutable as heaven's.

Here is no progress to sublimer life ;

Nature stands still, — stands at the very point,

Whence from a vantage-ground her bolder steps

Might rise resplendent on the scale of being ;

Rank over rank, awakening with her tread,

Inquisitive, intelligent ; aspiring,

Each above other, all above themselves,

Till every generation should transcend

The former, as the former all the past.

" Such, such alone were meet inhabitants

For these fair isles, so wonderfully form'd

Amidst the solitude of sea and sky,

On which my wandering spirit first was cast,

And still beyond whose girdle, eye nor wing

Can carry me to undiscover'd climes,

Where many a nobler race may dwell ; whose waifs

And exiles, toss'd by tempests on the flood,

Hither might drift upon their native trees ;

Or, like their own free birds, on fearless pinions,

Make voyages amidst the pathless heaven,

And, lighting, colonize these fertile tracts,

Recover'd from the barrenness of ocean,

Whose wealth might well repay the brave adventure.

— Hath nature spent her strength ? Why stopp'd

   she here?

Why stopp'd not lower, if to rise no higher ?

Can she not summon from more ancient regions,

Beyond the rising or the setting sun,

Creatures, as far above the mightiest here

As yonder eagle, flaming at high noon,

Outsoars the bat that flutters through the twilight ?

Or as the tender Pelican excels

The anomalous abortion of the rock,

In which plant, fossil, animal unite ?

" But changes here may happen – changes must !

What hinders that new shores should yet ascend

Out of the bosom of the deep, and spread

Till all converge, from one circumference,

Into a solid breadth of table-land,

Bound by the horizon, canopied with heaven,

And ocean in his own abyss absorb'd ? "

While these imaginations cross'd the mind,

My thoughts fulfill'd themselves before mine eyes ;

The islands moved like circles upon water,

Expanding till they touch'd each other, closed

The interjacent straits, and thus became

A spacious continent which fill'd the sea.

That change was total, like a birth, a death ;

— Birth, that from native darkness brings to light

The young inhabitant of this gay world ;

Death, that from seen to unseen things removes,

And swallows time up in eternity.

That which had been, for ever ceased to be,

And that which follow'd was a new creation

Wrought from the disappearance of the old.

So fled that pageant universe away,

With all its isles and waters. So I found

Myself translated to that other world,

By sleight of fancy, like the unconscious act

Of waking from a pleasant dream, with sweet

Relapse into a more transporting vision.

The nursery of brooding Pelicans,

The dormitory of their dead, had vanish'd,

And all the minor spots of rock and verdure,

The abodes of happy millions, were no more :

But in their place a shadowy landscape lay,

On whose extremest western verge, a gleam

Of living silver, to the downward sun

Intensely glittering, mark'd the boundary line,

Which ocean, held by chains invisible,

Fretted and foam'd in vain to overleap.

Woods, mountains, valleys, rivers, glens, and plains

Diversified the scene : — that scene was wild,

Magnificent, deform'd, or beautiful,

As framed expressly for all kinds of life,

With all life's labours, sufferings, and enjoyments ;

Untouch'd as yet by any meaner hand

Than His who made it, and pronounced it good.

And good it was ; — free as light, air, fire, water,

To every thing that breathed upon its surface,

From the small worm that crept abroad at midnight

To sip cool dews and feed on sleeping flowers,

Then slunk into its hole, the little vampire !

Through every species which I yet had seen,

To animals, of tribes and forms unknown

In the lost islands ; — beasts that ranged the forests,

Grazed in the valleys, bounded o'er the hills,

Reposed in rich savannahs, from grey rocks

Pick'd the thin herbage sprouting through their fis-
    sures ;

Or in waste howling deserts found oases,

And fountains pouring sweeter streams than nectar,

And more melodious than the nightingale,

— So to the faint and perishing they seem'd.

I gazed on ruminating herds of kine,

And sheep for ever wandering ; goats that swung

Like spiders on the crags, so slight their hold ;

Deer, playful as their fawns, in peace, but fell

As battling bulls in wars of jealousy :

Through flowery champaigns roam'd the fleet gazelles,

Of many a colour, size, and shape, — all graceful ;

In every look, step, attitude prepared,

Even at the shadow of a cloud, to vanish,

And leave a solitude where thousands stood,

With heads declined, and nibbling eagerly

As locusts when they light on some new soil,

And move no more till they have shorn it bare.

On these, with famine unappeasable,

Lithe, muscular, huge-boned, and limb'd for leaping,

The brindled tyrants of brute nature prey'd :

The weak and timid bow'd before the strong,

The many by the few were hourly slaughter'd,

Where power was right, and violence was law.

   Here couch'd the panting tiger, on the watch ;

Impatient but unmoved, his fire-ball eyes

Made horrid twilight in the sunless jungle,

Till on the heedless buffalo he sprang,

Dragg'd the low-bellowing monster to his lair,

Crash'd through the ribs at once into its heart,

Quaff'd the hot blood, and gorged the quivering flesh,

Till drunk he lay as powerless as the carcass.

There, to the solitary lion's roar

So many echoes answer'd, that there seem'd

Ten in the field for one ; — where'er they turn'd,

The flying animals, from cave to cave,

Heard his voice issuing ; and recoil'd aghast,

Only to meet it nearer than before,

Or, ere they saw his shadow or his face,

Fall dead beneath his thunder-striking paw.

Calm amidst scenes of havoc, in his own

Huge strength impregnable, the elephant

Offended none, but led his quiet life

Among his old contemporary trees,

Till Nature laid him gently down to rest

Beneath the palm, which he was wont to make

His prop in slumber ; there his relics lay

Longer than life itself had dwelt within them.

Bees in the ample hollow of his scull

Piled their wax-citadels, and stored their honey ;

Thence sallied forth to forage through the fields,

And swarm'd in emigrating legions thence :

There, little burrowing animals threw up

Hillocks beneath the overarching ribs ;

While birds, within the spinal labyrinth,

Contrived their nests : — so wandering Arabs pitch

Their tents amidst Palmyra's palaces ;

So Greek and Roman peasants build their huts

Beneath the shadow of the Parthenon,

Or on the ruins of the Capitol.

But unintelligent creation soon

Fail'd to delight ; the novelty departed,

And all look'd desolate ; my eye grew weary

Of seeing that which it might see for ever

Without a new idea or emotion ;

The mind within me panted after mind,

The spirit sigh'd to meet a kindred spirit,

And in my human heart there was a void,

Which nothing but humanity could fill.

At length, as though a prison-door were open'd,

Chains had fall'n off, and by an angel-guide

Conducted, I escaped that desert-bourne ;

And instantaneously I travell'd on,

Yet knew not how, for wings nor feet I plied,

But with a motion, like the lapse of thought,

O'er many a vale and mountain I was carried,

Till in the east, above the ocean's brim,

I saw the morning sun, and stay'd my course,

Where vestiges of rude but social life

Arrested and detain'd attention long.

    Amidst the crowd of grovelling animals,

A being more majestic stood before me ;

I met an eye that look'd into my soul,

And seem'd to penetrate mine inmost thoughts.

Instinctively I turn'd away to hide them,

For shame and quick compunction came upon me,

As though detected on forbidden ground,

Gazing on things unlawful : but my heart

Relented quickly, and my bosom throbb'd

With such unutterable tenderness,

That every sympathy of human nature

Was by the beating of a pulse enkindled,

And flash'd at once throughout the mind's recesses,

As in a darken'd chamber, objects start

All round the walls, the moment light breaks in.

The sudden tumult of surprise awoke

My spirit from that trance of vague abstraction,

Wherein I lived through ages, and beheld

Their generations pass so swiftly by me,

That years were moments in their flight, and hours

The scenes of crowded centuries reveal'd ;

I sole spectator of the wondrous changes,

Spell-bound as in a dream, and acquiescing

In all that happen'd, though perplex'd with strange

Conceit of something wanting through the whole.

That spell was broken, like the vanish'd film

From eyes born blind, miraculously open'd ; —

'Twas gone, and I became myself again,

Restored to memory of all I knew

From books or schools, the world or sage experience ;

With all that folly or misfortune taught me, —

Each hath her lessons, — wise are they that learn.

Still the mysterious revery went on,

And I was still sole witness of its issues,

But with clear mind and disenchanted sight,

Beholding, judging, comprehending all ;

Not passive and bewilder'd as before.

What was the being which I then beheld ?

Man going forth amidst inferior creatures :

Not as he rose in Eden out of dust,

Fresh from the moulding hand of Deity ;

Immortal breath upon his lips ; the light

Of uncreated glory in his soul ;

Lord of the nether universe, and heir

Of all above him, — all above the sky,

The sapphire pavement of his future palace :

Not so ; — but rather like that morning-star,

Which from the highest empyrean fell

Into the bottomless abyss of darkness ;

There flaming only with malignant beams

Among the constellations of his peers,

The third part of heaven's host, with him cast down

To irretrievable perdition, — thence,

Amidst the smoke of unillumined fires,

Issuing like horrid sparks to blast creation :

— Thus, though in dim eclipse, before me stood,

As from a world invisible call'd up,

Man, in the image of his Maker form'd,

Man, to the image of his tempter fall'n ;

Yet still as far above infernal fiends,

As once a little lower than the angels.

I knew him, own'd him, loved him, and exclaim'd,

" Bone of my bone, flesh of my flesh, my Brother !

Hail in the depth of thy humiliation ;

For dear thou art, amidst unconscious ruin, —

Dear to the kindliest feelings of my soul,

As though one womb had borne us, and one mother

At her sweet breasts had nourish'd us as twins. "

I saw him sunk in loathsome degradation,

A naked, fierce, ungovernable savage,

Companion to the brutes, himself more brutal ;

Superior only in the craft that made

The serpent subtlest beast of all the field,

Whose guile unparadised the world, and brought

A curse upon the earth which God had blessed.

That curse was here, without the mitigation

Of healthful toil, that half redeems the ground

Whence man was taken, whither he returns,

And which repays him bread for patient labour,

— Labour, the symbol of his punishment,

— Labour, the secret of his happiness.

The curse was here ; for thorns and briars o'erran

The tangled labyrinths, yet briars bare roses,

And thorns threw out their annual snow of blossoms :

The curse was here ; and yet the soil untill'd

Pour'd forth spontaneous and abundant harvests,

Pulse and small berries, maize in strong luxuriance,

And slender rice that grew by many waters ;

The forests cast their fruits, in husk or rind,

Yielding sweet kernels or delicious pulp,

Smooth oil, cool milk, and unfermented wine,

In rich and exquisite variety.

On these the indolent inhabitants

Fed without care or forethought, like the swine

That grubb'd the turf, and taught them where to

    look

For dainty earth-nuts and nutritious roots ;

Or the small monkeys, capering on the boughs,

And rioting on nectar and ambrosia,

The produce of that Paradise run wild : —

No, — these were merry, if they were not wise ;

While man's untutor'd hordes were sour and sullen,

Like those abhorr'd baboons, whose gluttonous taste

They follow'd safely in their choice of food ;

And whose brute semblance of humanity

Made them more hideous than their prototypes,

That bore the genuine image and inscription,

Defaced indeed, but yet indelible.

— From ravening beasts, and fowls that fish'd the

    ocean,

Men learn'd to prey on meaner animals,

But found a secret out which birds or beasts,

Most cruel, cunning, treacherous, never knew,

— The luxury of devouring one another.

Such were my kindred in their lost estate,

From whose abominations while I turn'd,

As from a pestilence, I mourn'd and wept

With bitter lamentation o'er their ruin ;

Sunk as they were in ignorance of all

That raises man above his origin,

And elevates to heaven the spirit within him,

To which the Almighty's breath gave understanding.

Large was their stature, and their frames athletic ;

Their skins were dark, their locks like eagles' feathers ;

Their features terrible ; — when roused to wrath,

All evil passions lighten'd through their eyes,

Convulsed their bosoms like possessing fiends,

And loosed what sets on fire the course of nature,

— The tongue of malice, set on fire of hell,

Which then, in cataracts of horrid sounds,

Raged through their gnashing teeth and foaming lips,

Making the ear to tingle, and the soul

Sicken, with spasms of strange revolting horror,

As if the blood changed colour in the veins,

While hot and cold it ran about the heart,

And red to pale upon the cheek it shew'd.

Their visages at rest were winter-clouds,

Fix'd gloom, whence sun nor shower could be foretold:

But, in high revelry, when full of prey,

Cannibal prey, tremendous was their laughter ;

Their joy, the shock of earthquakes overturning

Mountains, and swamping rivers in their course ;

Or subterranean elements embroil'd, —

Wind, fire, and water, till the cleft volcano

Gives to their devastating fury vent :

That joy was lurking hatred in disguise,

And not less fatal in its last excess.

They danced, — like whirlwinds in the Libyan waste,

When the dead sand starts up in living pillars,

That mingle, part, and cross, then burst in ruin

On man and beast ; — they danced to shouts and
    screams,

Drums, gongs, and horns, their deafening din inflicting

On nerves and ears enraptured with such clangour ;

Till mirth grew madness, and the feast a fray,

That left the field strown with unnatural carnage,

To furnish out a more unnatural feast,

And lay the train to inflame a bloodier fray.

    They dwelt in dens and caverns of the earth,

Won by the valiant from their brute possessors,

And held in hourly peril of reprisals

From the ferocious brigands of the woods.

The lioness, benighted with her whelps,

There seeking shelter from the drenching storm,

Met with unseen resistance on the threshold,

And perish'd ere she knew by what she fell ;

Or, finding all within asleep, surprised

The inmates in their dreams, from which no more

Her deadly vengeance suffer'd them to wake.

— On open plains they framed low, narrow huts

Of boughs, the wreck of windfalls or of Time,

Wattled with canes, and thatch'd with reeds and
    leaves ;

There from afflictive noon sought twilight shadow,

Or slumber'd in the smoke of greenwood fires,

To drive away the pestilent musquitos.

— Some built unwieldy nests among the trees,

In which to doze by night, or watch by day

The joyful moment, from that ambuscade

To slay the passing antelope, or wound

The jackal chasing it, with sudden arrows

From bows that task'd a giant's strength to bend.

In flight or combat, on the champaign field,

They ran atilt with flinty-headed spears ;

Or launch'd the lighter javelin through the air,

Follow'd its motion with a basilisk's eye,

And shriek'd with gladness when a life was spill'd :

They sent the pebble hissing from the sling,

Hot as the curse from lips that would strike dead,

If words were stones ; here stones, as swift as words

Can reach the ear, the unwary victim smote.

In closer conflict, breast to breast, when one

Or both must perish on the spot, they fought

With clubs of iron-wood and ponderous force,

Wielded with terrible dexterity,

And falling down like thunderbolts, which nought

But counter-thunderbolts could meet or parry.

Rude-fashion'd weapons ! yet the lion's jaws,

The tiger's grasp, the eagle's beak and talons,

The serpent's fangs, were not more formidable,

More sure to hit, or, hitting, sure to kill.

They knew not shame nor honour, yet knew pride ;

— The pride of strength, skill, speed, and subtlety ;

The pride of tyranny and violence,

Not o'er the mighty only, whom their arm

Had crush'd in battle, or had basely slain

By treacherous ambush, or more treacherous smiles,

Embracing while they stabb'd the heart that met

Their specious seeming with unguarded breast :

— The reckless savages display'd their pride

By vile oppression in its vilest forms, —

Oppression of the weak and innocent ;

Infancy, womanhood, old age, disease,

The lame, the halt, the blind, were wrong'd, neglected,

Exposed to perish by wild beasts in woods,

Cast to the crocodiles in rivers ; murder'd

Even by their dearest kindred in cold blood,

To rid themselves of Nature's gracious burthens,

In mercy laid on man to teach *him* mercy.

But their prime glory was insane debauch,

To inflict and bear excruciating tortures ;

The unshrinking victim, while the flesh was rent

From his live limbs, and eaten in his presence,

Still in his death-pangs taunted his tormentors

With tales of cruelty more diabolic,

Wreak'd by himself upon the friends of those

Who now their impotence of vengeance wasted

On him, and drop by drop his life extorted

With thorns and briers of the wilderness,

Or the slow violence of untouching fire.

    Vanity too, pride's mannikin, here play'd

Satanic tricks to ape her master-fiend.

The leopard's beauteous spoils, the lion's mane,

Engirt the loins, and waved upon the shoulders

Of those whose wiles or arms had won such trophies :

Rude-punctured figures of all loathsome things,

Toads, scorpions, asps, snakes' eyes and double

    tongues,

In flagrant colours on their tattooed limbs,

Gave proof of intellect, not dead but sleeping,

And in its trance enacting strange vagaries.

Bracelets of human teeth, fangs of wild beasts,

The jaws of sharks, and beaks of ravenous birds,

Glitter'd and tinkled round their arms and ankles ;

While skulls of slaughter'd enemies, in chains

Of natural elf-locks, dangled from the necks

Of those, whose own bare skulls and cannibal teeth

Ere long must deck more puissant fiends than they.

On ocean, too, they exercised dominion : —

Of hollow trees composing slight canoes,

They paddled o'er the reefs, cut through the breakers,

And rode the untamed billows far from shore ;

Amphibious from their infancy, and fearing

Nought in the deepest waters save the shark ;

Even him, well arm'd, they gloried to encounter,

And when he turn'd to ope those gates of death,

That led into the Hades of his gorge,

Smote with such stern decision to his vitals,

And vanish'd through the blood-beclouded waves,

That, blind and desperate in his agony,

Headlong he plunged and perish'd in the abyss.

Woman was here the powerless slave of man ;

Thus fallen Adam tramples fallen Eve,

Through all the generations of his sons,

In whose barbarian veins the old serpent's venom

Turns pure affection into hideous lust,

And wrests the might of his superior arm

(Given to defend and bless his meek companion)

Into the very yoke and scourge of bondage ;

Till limbs, by beauty moulded, eyes of gladness,

And the full bosom of confiding truth,

Made to delight and comfort him in toil,

And change care's den into a halcyon's nest,

— Are broke with drudgery, quench'd with stagnant

tears,

Or wrung with lonely unimparted woe.

Man is beside himself, not less than fall'n

Below his dignity, who owns not woman

As nearer to his heart than when she grew

A rib within him, — as his heart's own heart.

He slew the game with his unerring arrow,

But left it in the bush for her to drag

Home, with her feeble hands, already burthen'd

With a young infant clinging to her shoulders.

Here she fell down in travail by the way,

Her piteous groans unheard, or heard unanswer'd ;

There, with her convoy, she – mother, and child,

And slaughter'd deer, — became some wild beast's

    prey ;

Though spoils so rich not one could long enjoy, —

Soon the woods echoed with the huge uproar

Of savage throats contending for the bodies,

Till not a bone was left for farther quarrel.

— He chose the spot ; she piled the wood, she wove

The supple withes, and bound the thatch that form'd

The ground-built cabin or the tree-swung nest.

— He brain'd the drowsy panther in his den,

At noon o'ercome by heat, and with closed lids

Fearing assaults from none but vexing flies,

Which with his ring-streak'd tail he switch'd away :

The citadel thus storm'd, the monster slain,

By the dread prowess of his daring arm,

She roll'd the stones, and planted the stockade,

To fortify the garrison for him,

Who scornfully look'd on, at ease reclined,

Or only rose to beat her to the task.

Yet, 'midst the gall and wormwood of her lot,

She tasted joys which none but woman knows,

— The hopes, fears, feelings, raptures of a mother,

Well-nigh compensating for his unkindness,

Whom yet with all her fervent soul she loved.

Dearer to her than all the universe,

The looks, the cries, the embraces of her babes ;

In each of whom she lived a separate life,

And felt the fountain, whence their veins were fill'd,

Flow in perpetual union with the streams,

That swell'd their pulses, and throbb'd back through

    hers.

Oh ! 'twas benign relief when my vex'd eye

Could turn from man, the sordid, selfish savage,

And gaze on woman in her self-denial,

To him and to their offspring all alive,

Dead only to herself, — save when she won

His unexpected smile ; then, then she look'd

A thousand times more beautiful, to meet

A glance of aught like tenderness from him ;

And sent the sunshine of her happy heart

So warm into the charnel-house of his,

That Nature's genuine sympathies awoke,

And he almost forgot himself in her.

O man ! Lost man ! amidst the desolation

Of goodness in thy soul, there yet remains

One spark of Deity, — that spark is love.

THE

PELICAN ISLAND.

CANTO SEVENTH.

AGES again, with silent revolution,

Brought morn and even, noon and night, with all

The old vicissitudes of Nature's aspect :

Rains in their season fertilized the ground,

Winds sow'd the seeds of every kind of plant

On its peculiar soil ; while suns matured

What winds had sown, and rains in season water'd,

Providing nourishment for all that lived :

Man's generations came and went like these,

— The grass and flowers that wither where they spring;

— The brutes that perish wholly where they fall.

Thus while I mused on these in long succession,

And all remained as all had been before,

I cried, as I was wont, though none did listen,

— 'Tis sweet sometimes to speak and be the hearer ;

For he is twice himself who can converse

With his own thoughts, as with a living throng

Of fellow-travellers in solitude ;

And mine too long had been my sole companions :

— " What is this mystery of human life ?

In rude or civilized society,

Alike, a pilgrim's progress through this world

To that which is to come, by the same stages ;

With infinite diversity of fortune

To each distinct adventurer by the way !

" Life is the transmigration of a soul

Through various bodies, various states of being ;

New manners, passions, tastes, pursuits in each ;

In nothing, save in consciousness, the same.

Infancy, adolescence, manhood, age,

Are alway moving onward, alway losing

Themselves in one another, lost at length,

Like undulations, on the strand of death.

The sage of threescore years and ten looks back, —

With many a pang of lingering tenderness,

And many a shuddering conscience-fit, — on what

He hath been, is not, cannot be again ;

Nor trembles less with fear and hope, to think

What he is now, but cannot long continue,

And what he must be through uncounted ages.

— The Child ; — we know no more of happy childhood,

Than happy childhood knows of wretched eld ;

And all our dreams of its felicity

Are incoherent as its own crude visions :

We but begin to live from that fine point

Which memory dwells on, with the morning-star,

The earliest note we heard the cuckoo sing,

Or the first daisy that we ever pluck'd,

When thoughts themselves were stars, and birds, and
    flowers,

Pure brilliance, simplest music, wild perfume.

Thenceforward, mark the metamorphoses !

— The Boy, the Girl ; — when all was joy, hope,

  promise ;

Yet who would be a Boy, a Girl again,

To bear the yoke, to long for liberty,

And dream of what will never come to pass ?

— The Youth, the Maiden ; — living but for love,

Yet learning soon that life hath other cares,

And joys less rapturous, but more enduring :

— The Woman ; — in her offspring multiplied ;

A tree of life, whose glory is her branches,

Beneath whose shadow, she (both root and stem)

Delights to dwell in meek obscurity,

That they may be the pleasure of beholders :

Whose birth requires his death to make them room,

Yet in whose lives he feels his resurrection,

And grows immortal in his children's children :

— Then the grey Elder ; — leaning on his staff,

And bow'd beneath a weight of years, that steal

Upon him with the secrecy of sleep,

(No snow falls lighter than the snow of age,

None with such subtlety benumbs the frame)

Till he forgets sensation, and lies down

Dead in the lap of his primeval mother ;

She throws a shroud of turf and flowers around him,

Then calls the worms, and bids them do their office :

— Man giveth up the ghost, — and where is He ?"

That startling question broke my lucubration ;

I saw those changes realized before me ;

Saw them recurring in perpetual line,

The line unbroken, while the thread ran on,

Failing at this extreme, at that renew'd,

— Like buds, leaves, blossoms, fruits on herbs and
  trees ;
Like mites, flies. Reptiles ; birds, and beasts, and
  fishes,
Of every length of period here, — all mortal,
And all resolved into those elements
Whence they had emanated, whence they drew
Their sustenance, and which their wrecks recruited
To generate and foster other forms
As like themselves as were the lights of heaven,
For ever moving in serene succession,
— Not like those lights unquenchable by time,
But ever changing, like the clouds that come,
Who can tell whence? and go, who can tell whither?
Thus the swift series of man's race elapsed,
As for no higher destiny created
Than aught beneath them, — from the elephant

Down to the worm, thence to the zoophyte,

That link which binds Prometheus to his rock,

The living fibre to insensate matter.

They were not, then they were ; the unborn, the

    living !

They were, then were not ; they had lived and died ;

No trace, no record of their date remaining,

Save in the memory of kindred beings,

Themselves as surely hastening to oblivion ;

Till, where the soil had been renew'd by relics,

And earth, air, water were one sepulchre,

Earth, air, and water might be search'd in vain,

Atom by atom scrutinized with eyes

Of microscopic power, that could discern

The population of a dew-drop, yet

No particle betray the buried secret

Of what they had been, or of what they were :

Life thus was swallow'd by mortality,

Mortality thus swallow'd up of life,

And man remain'd the world's unmoved possessor,

Though every moment men appear'd and vanish'd.

Oh ! 'twas heart-sickness to behold them thus

Perishing without knowledge ; — perishing,

As though they were but things of dust and ashes.

They lived unconscious of their noblest powers,

As were the rocks and mountains which they trod

Of gold and jewels hidden in their bowels ;

They lived unconscious of what lived within them,

The deathless spirit, as were the stars that shone

Above their heads, of their own emanations.

And did it live within them ? did there dwell

Fire brought from heaven in forms of miry clay ?

Untemper'd as the slime of Babel's builders,

And left unfinish'd like their monstrous work ?

To me, alas ! they seem'd but living bodies,

With still-born souls which never could be quicken'd,

Till death brought immortality to light,

And from the darkness of their earthly prison

Placed them at once before the bar of God ;

Then first to learn, at their eternal peril,

The fact of his existence and their own.

Imagination durst not follow them,

Nor stand one moment at that dread tribunal.

" Shall not the Judge of all the earth do right ?"

I trembled while I spake. I could not bear

The doubt, fear, horror, that o'erhung the fate

Of millions, millions, millions, — living, dying,

Without a hope to hang a hope upon,

That of the whole it might not be affirm'd,

— "Twere better that they had never been born."

I turn'd away, and look'd for consolation,

Where Nature else had shrunk with loathing back,

Or imprecated curses, in her wrath,

Even on the fallen creatures of my race,

O'er whose mysterious doom my heart was breaking.

   I saw an idiot with long haggard visage,

And eye of vacancy, trolling his tongue

From cheek to cheek ; then muttering syllables,

Which all the learned on earth could not interpret ;

Yet were they sounds of gladness, tones of pleasure,

Ineffable tranquillity expressing,

Or pure and buoyant animal-delight :

For bright the sun shone round him ; cool the breeze

Play'd in the floating shadow of the palm,

Where he lay rolling in voluptuous sloth :

And he had fed deliciously on fruit,

That fell into his lap, and virgin honey,

That melted from the hollow of the rock,

Whither the hum and stir of bees had drawn him.

He knew no bliss beside, save sleep when weary,

Or reveries like this, when broad awake.

Glimpses of thought seem'd flashing through his
  brain,

Like wildfires flitting o'er the rank morass,

Snares to the night-bewilder'd traveller !

Gently he raised his head, and peep'd around,

As if he hoped to see some pleasant object,

— The wingless squirrel jet from tree to tree,

— The monkey pilfering a parrot's nest

But, ere he bore the precious spoil away

Surprised behind by beaks, and wings, and claws,

That made him scamper gibbering away ;

— The sly opossum dangle by her tail,

To snap the silly birds that perch'd too near ;

Or in the thicket, with her young at play,

Start when the rustling grass announced a snake,

And secrete them within her second womb,

Then stand alert to give the intruder battle,

Who rear'd his crest, and hiss'd, and glid away : —

— These with the transport of a child he view'd,

Then laugh'd aloud, and crack'd his fingers, smote

His palms, and clasp'd his knees, convulsed with glee ;

A sad, sad spectacle of merriment !

Yet he was happy ; happy in this life ;

And could I doubt, that death to him would bring

Intelligence, which he had ne'er abused,

A soul, which he had never lost by sin ?

  I saw a woman, panting from her throes,

Stretch'd in a lonely cabin on the ground,

Pale with the anguish of her bitter hour,

Whose sorrow she forgat not in the joy,

Which mothers feel when a man-child is born ;

Hers was an infant of her own scorn'd sex :

It lay upon her breast ; — she laid it there,

By the same instinct, which taught it to find

The milky fountain, fill'd to meet its wants

Even at the gate of life, — to drink and live.

Awhile she lay all-passive to the touch

Of those small fingers, and the soft, soft lips

Soliciting the sweet nutrition thence,

While yearning sympathy crept round her heart :

She felt her spirit yielding to the charm,

That wakes the parent in the fellest bosom,

And binds her to her little one for ever,

If once completed ; — but she broke, she broke it.

For she was brooding o'er her sex's wrongs,

And seem'd to lie amidst a nest of scorpions,

That stung remorse to frenzy : — forth she sprang,

And with collected might a moment stood,

Mercy and misery struggling in her thoughts,

Yet both impelling her to one dire purpose.

There was a little grave already made,

But two spans long, in the turf-floor beside her,

By him who was the father of that child :

Thence he had sallied, when the work was done,

To hunt, to fish, or ramble on the hills,

Till all was peace again within that dwelling,

— His haunt, his den, his any thing but home !

Peace ? — no, till the new-comer were dispatch'd

Whence it should ne'er return, to break the stupor

Of unawaken'd conscience in himself.

    She pluck'd the baby from her flowing breast,

And o'er its mouth, yet moist with Nature's beverage,

Bound a thick lotus-leaf to still its cries ;

Then laid it down in that untimely grave,

As tenderly as though 'twere rock'd to sleep

With songs of love, and she afraid to wake it :

Soon as she felt it touch the ground, she started,

Hurried the damp earth over it ; then fell

Flat on the heaving heap, and crush'd it down

With the whole burthen of her grief ; exclaiming,

" O that my mother had done so to me ! "

Then in a swoon forgot, a little while,

Her child, her sex, her tyrant, and herself.

    Amazement wither'd up all human feeling ;

I wonder'd how I could look on so calmly,

As though I were but animated stone,

And not kneel down upon the spot, and pray

That earth might open to devour that mother,

Or heaven shoot lightning to avenge that daughter :

But horror soon gave way to hope and pity,

— Hope for the dead, and pity for the living.

Thenceforth when I beheld troops of wild children

Frolicking round the tents of wickedness,

Though my heart danced within me to the music

Of their loud voices and unruly mirth,

The blithe exuberance of beginning life !

I could not weep when they went out like sparks,

That glitter, creep, and dwindle out, on tinder.

Happy, thrice happy were they thus to die,

Rather than grow into such men and women,

— Such fiends incarnate as that felon-sire,

Who dug its grave before his child was born ;

Such miserable wretches as that mother,

Whose tender mercies were so deadly cruel !

I saw their infant's spirit rise to heaven,

Caught from its birth up to the throne of God ;

There, thousands and ten thousands, I beheld,

Of innocents like this, that died untimely,

By violence of their unnatural kin,

Or by the mercy of that gracious Power,

Who gave them being, taking what He gave

Ere they could sin or suffer like their parents.

I saw them in white raiment, crown'd with flowers,

On the fair banks of that resplendent river,

Whose streams make glad the city of our God ;

— Water of life, as clear as crystal, welling

Forth from the throne itself, and visiting

Fields of a Paradise that ne'er was lost ;

Where yet the tree of life immortal grows,

And bears its monthly fruits, twelve kinds of fruit,

Each in its season, food of saints and angels ;

Whose leaves are for the healing of the nations.

Beneath the shadow of its blessed boughs,

I mark'd those rescued infants, in their schools,

By spirits of just men made perfect, taught

The glorious lessons of almighty love,

Which brought them thither by the readiest path

From the world's wilderness of dire temptations,

Securing thus their everlasting weal.

Yea, in the rapture of that hour, though songs

Of cherubim to golden lyres and trumpets,

And the redeem'd upon the sea of glass,

With voices like the sound of many waters,

Came on mine ear, whose secret cells were open'd

To entertain celestial harmonies,

— The small, sweet accents of those little children,

Pouring out all the gladness of their souls

In love, joy, gratitude, and praise to Him,

— Him, who had loved and wash'd them in his blood ;

These were to me the most transporting strains,

Amidst the hallelujahs of all heaven. —

Though lost awhile in that amazing chorus

Around the throne, — at happy intervals,

The shrill hosannas of the infant-choir,

Singing in that eternal temple, brought

Tears to mine eye, which seraphs had been glad

To weep, could they have felt the sympathy

That melted all my soul, when I beheld

How condescending Deity thus deign'd,

Out of the mouths of babes and sucklings here,

To perfect his high praise : — the harp of heaven

Had lack'd its least but not its meanest string,

Had children not been taught to play upon it,

And sing, from feelings all their own, what men

Nor angels can conceive of creatures, born

Under the curse, yet from the curse redeem'd,

And placed at once beyond the power to fall,

— Safety which men nor angels ever knew,

Till ranks of these and all of those had fallen.

THE

PELICAN ISLAND.

CANTO EIGHTH.

'Twas but the vision of an eye-glance ; gone

Ere thought could fix upon it, — gone like lightning

At midnight, when the expansive flash reveals

Alps, Appenines and Pyrenees, in one

Glorious horizon, suddenly lit up, —

Rocks, rivers, forests, — quench'd as suddenly :

A glimpse that fill'd the mind with images,

Which years cannot obliterate ; but stamp'd

With instantaneous everlasting force

On memory's more than adamantine tablet ; —

A glimpse of that which eye hath never seen,

Ear heard, nor heart of man conceived. – It pass'd,

But what it shew'd can never pass. — It pass'd,

And left me wandering through that land of exile,

Cut off from intercourse with happier lands ;

Abandon'd, as it seem'd, by its Creator ;

Unvisited by Him, who came from heaven

To seek and save the lost of every clime ;

And where God, looking down in wrath, had said,

" My spirit shall no longer strive with man : "

— So ignorance or unbelief might deem.

Was it thus outlaw'd ? No ; God left himself

Not without witness of his presence there ;

He gave them rain from heaven and fruitful seasons,

Filling unthankful hearts with food and gladness.

He gave them kind affections which they strangled,

Turning his grace into lasciviousness.

He gave them powers of intellect, to scale

Heaven's height ; to name and number all the stars ;

To penetrate earth's depths for hidden riches,

Or clothe its surface with fertility ;

Amidst the haunts of dragons, dens of satyrs,

To call up hamlets, villages, and towns,

The abode of peace and industry ; to build

Cities and palaces amid waste places ;

To sound the ocean, combat with the winds,

Travel the waves, and compass every shore,

On voyages of commerce or adventure ;

To shine in civil and refining arts,

With tranquil science elevate the soul ;

To explore the universe of mind ; to trace

The Nile of thinking to its secret source,

And thence pursue its infinite meanders,

Not lost amidst the labyrinths of Time,

But o'er the cataract of death down rolling,

To flow for ever, and for ever, and for ever,

Where time nor space can limit its expansion.

And live, amidst the daylight of this world,

In regions of enchantment ; — with the force

Of song, as with a spirit, to possess

The souls of those that hearken, till they feel

But what the minstrel feels, and do but that,

Which his strange inspiration makes them do ;

Thus with his breath to kindle war, and bring

The array of battle to electric issue ;

Or, while opposing legions, front to front,

Wait the dread signal for the work of havoc,

Step in between, and with the healing voice

Of harmony and concord win them so,

That hurling down their weapons of destruction,

They rush into each other's arms, with shouts

And tears of transport ; till inveterate foes

Are friends and brethren, feasting on the field,

Where vultures else had feasted, and gorged wolves

Howl'd in convulsive slumber o'er their corses.

    Such powers to these were given, but given in vain ;

They knew them not, or, as they learn'd to know,

Perverted them to more pernicious evil,

Than ignorance had skill to perpetrate.

Yet the great Father gave a richer portion

To these, the most impoverish'd of his children ;

He sent the light that lighteth every man,

That comes into the world, — the light of truth :

But Satan turn'd that light to darkness ; turn'd

God's truth into a lie, and they believed

His lie, who led them captive at his will,

Usurp'd the throne of Deity on earth,

And claim'd allegiance, in all hideous forms,

— The abominable emblems of himself,

The legion-fiend, who takes whatever shape

Man's crazed imagination can devise

To body forth his notion of a God,

And prove how low immortal minds can fall,

When from the living God they fall, to serve

Dumb idols. Thus they worshipp'd stocks and stones,

Which hands unapt for sculpture executed,

In their egregious folly, like themselves,

Though not more like, even in barbarian eyes,

Than antic clouds resemble animals.

To these they offer'd flowers and fruits ; to those,

Reptiles ; to others, birds, and beasts, and fishes ;

To some they sacrificed their enemies,

To more their children, and themselves to all.

So had the god of this apostate world

Blinded their eyes. But the true God had placed

Yet further witness of his grace among them,

When all remembrance of himself was lost :

— Knowledge of good and evil, right and wrong ;

But knowledge was confounded, till they call'd

Good evil, evil good ; refused the right,

And chose and loved the wrong for its own sake.

One witness more, his own ambassador

On earth, the Almighty left to be their prophet,

Whom Satan could not utterly beguile,

Nor always hold with his ten thousand fetters,

Lock'd in the dungeon of the obdurate breast,

And trampled down by all its atheist inmates ;

— Conscience, tremendous conscience, in his fits

Of inspiration, — whencesoe'er it came, —

Rose like a ghost, inflicting fear of death,

On those who fear'd not death in fiercest battle,

And mock'd him in their martyrdoms of torments :

That secret, swift, and silent messenger

Broke on them in their lonely hours, — in sleep,

In sickness ; haunting them with dire suspicions

Of something in themselves that would not die, —

Of an existence elsewhere, and hereafter,

Of which tradition was not wholly silent,

Yet spake not out ; its dreary oracles

Confounded superstition to conceive,

And baffled scepticism to reject :

— What fear of death is like the fear beyond it ?

But pangs like these were lucid intervals

In the delirium of the life they led,

And all unwelcome as returning reason,

Which through the chaos of a maniac's brain

Shoots gleams of light more terrible than darkness.

These sad misgivings of the smitten heart,

Wounded unseen by conscience from its ambush ;

These voices from eternity, that spake

To an eternity of soul within, —

Were quickly lull'd by riotous enjoyment,

Or lost in hurricanes of headlong passion.

They knew no higher, sought no happier state ;

Had no fine instinct of superior joys

Than those of sense ; no taste for sense refined

Above the gross necessities of nature,

Or outraged Nature's most unnatural cravings.

Why should they toil to make the earth bring forth,

When without toil she gave them all they wanted ?

The bread-fruit ripen'd, while they lay beneath

Its shadow in luxurious indolence ;

The cocoa fill'd its nuts with milk and kernels,

While they were sauntering on the shores and mountains ;

And while they slumber'd from their heavy meals,

In dead forgetfulness of life itself,

The fish were spawning in unsounded depths,

The birds were breeding in adjacent trees,

The game was fattening in delicious pastures,

Unplanted roots were thriving under ground,

To spread the tables of their future banquets !

Thus what the sires had been, the sons became,

And generations rose, continued, went,

Without memorial, — like the Pelicans

On that lone island, where they built their nests,

Nourish'd their young, and then lay down to die.

Hence through a thousand and a thousand years,

Man's history, in that region of oblivion,

Might be recorded in a page as small

As the brief legend of those Pelicans,

With one appalling, one sublime distinction,

(Sublime with horror, with despair appalling,)

— That Pelicans were not transgressors ; — Man,

Apostate from the womb, by blood a traitor.

Thus, while he rose by dignity of birth,

He sank in guilt and infamy below

Creatures, whose being was but lent, not given,

And, when the debt was due, reclaim'd for ever.

O enviable lot of innocence !

Their bliss and woe were only of this world :

Whate'er their lives had been, though born to suffer

Not less than to enjoy, their end was peace.

Man was immortal, yet he lived and died

As though there were no life, nor death, but this :

Alas ! what life or death may be hereafter,

He only knows who hath ordain'd them both ;

And they shall know who prove their truth for ever.

The thought was agony beyond endurance ;

" O thou, my brother Man !" again I cried,

" Would God, that I might live, might die for thee !

O could I take a form to meet thine eyes,

Invent a voice with words to reach thine ears ;

Or if my spirit might converse with thine,

And pour my thoughts, fears, feelings, through thy
    breast,

Unknown to thee whence came the strange intrusion !

How would my soul rejoice, rejoice with trembling,

To tell thee who thou art, and bring thee home,

— Poor prodigal, here watching swine, and fain

To glut thy hunger with the husks they feed on, —

Home to our Father's house, our Father's heart !

Both, both are open to receive thee, — come ;

O come ! – He hears not, heeds not, — O my brother !

That I might prophesy to thee, — to all

The millions of dry bones that fill this valley

Of darkness and despair ! – Alas ! alas !

Can these bones live ? – Lord God, Thou knowest.

    — Come

From the four winds of heaven, almighty breath,

Blow on these slain, and they shall live."

                                  I spake,

And turning from the mournful contemplation,

To seek refreshment for my weary spirit,

Amidst that peopled continent, the abode

Of misery which reach'd beyond this world,

I lighted on a solitary glen

(A peaceful refuge in a land of discord,)

Crown'd with steep rocks, whose hoary summits shone

Amid the blue unclouded element,

O'er the green woods, that, stretching down the hills,

Border'd the narrow champaign glade between,

Through which a clear and pebbly rill meander'd.

The song-birds caroll'd in the leafy shades,

Those of resplendent plumage flaunted round ;

High o'er the cliffs the sea-fowl soar'd or perch'd ;

The Pelican and Albatross were seen

In groups reposing on the northern ridge :

There was entire serenity above,

Beauty, tranquillity, delight below,

And every motion, sound, and sight were pleasing.

Rhinoceros nor wild bull pastured here ;

Lion nor tiger here shed innocent blood ;

The antelopes were grazing void of fear,

Their young in antic gambols ramping by ;

While goats, from precipice to precipice

Clamber'd, or hung, or vaulted through the air,

As if a thought convey'd them to and fro.

Harmony reign'd, as once ere man's creation,

When brutes were yet earth's sole inhabitants.

There were no human tracks nor dwellings there,

For 'twas a sanctuary from hurtful creatures,

And in the precincts of that happy dell

The absence of my species was a mercy :

Thence the declining sun withdrew his beams,

But left it lighted by a hundred peaks,

Glittering and golden, round the span of sky,

That seem'd the sapphire roof of one great temple,

Whose floor was emerald, and whose walls the hills ;

Where those that worshipp'd God, might worship Him

In spirit and in truth, without distraction.

Man's absence pleased me ; yet on man alone,

Man fallen, helpless, miserable man,

My thoughts, prayers, wishes, tears, and sorrows

    turn'd,

Howe'er I strove to drive away every remembrance :

Then I refrain'd no longer, but brake out,

— "Lord God, why hast Thou made all men in vain ?"

THE

PELICAN ISLAND.

CANTO NINTH.

THE countenance of one advanced in years,

The shape of one created to command,

The step of one accustom'd to be seen,

And follow'd with the reverence of all eyes,

Yet conscious here of utter solitude,

Came on me like an apparition, — whence

I knew not, — halfway down the vale already

Had he proceeded ere I caught his eye,

And in that mirror of intelligence,

By the sure divination of mine art,

Read the mute history of his former life,

And all the untold secrets of his bosom.

He was a chieftain of renown ; from youth

To green old age the glory of his tribe,

The terror of their enemies ; in war

An Alexander, and in peace an Alfred.

From morn to night he wont to wield the spear

With indefatigable arm, or watch

From eve till dawn in ambush for his quarry,

Human or brute ; not less in chase than fight,

For strength, skill, prowess, enterprise unrivall'd.

Fearless he grappled with the fell hyaena,

And held him strangling in the grasp of fate ;

He seized the she-bear's whelps, and when the dam,

With miserable cries and insane rage,

Pursued to rescue them, would turn and strike

One blow, but one, to break her heart for ever :

From sling and bow, he sent upon death-errands

The stone or arrow through the trackless air,

To overtake the fleetest foot, or lay

The loftiest pinion fluttering in the dust.

On the rough waves he eagerly embark'd,

Assail'd the stranded whale among the breakers,

Dart after dart with such sure aim implanting

In the huge carcass of the helpless victim,

That soon in blood and foam the monster breath'd

His last, and lay a hulk upon the reef ;

Thence floated by the rising tide, and tow'd

By a whole navy of canoes ashore.

But 'twas the hero's mind that made him great ;

His eye, his lip, his hand, were clothed in thunder :

Thrones, crowns, and sceptres give not more

    ascendance,

Back'd with arm'd legions, fortified with towers,

Than this imperial savage, all alone,

From Nature's pure beneficence derived.

Yet, when the hey-day of hot youth was over,

His soul grew gentle as the halcyon breeze,

Sent from the evening-sea to bless the shore,

After the fervours of a tropic noon ;

Nor less benign his influence than fresh showers

Upon the fainting wilderness, where bands

Of pilgrims, bound for Mecca, with their camels,

Lie down to die together in despair,

When the deceitful *mirage*, that appear'd

A pool of water trembling in the sun,

Hath vanish'd from the bloodshot eye of thirst.

Firm in defence as valiant in the battle,

Assailing none, but all assaults repelling

With such determined chastisement, that foes

No longer dar'd to forage on his borders,

War shrunk from his dominions ; simple laws,

Yet wise and equitable, he ordain'd

To rule a willing and obedient people.

Blood ceased to flow in sacrifice ; no more

The parents' hands were raised against their children,

Children no longer slew their aged parents ;

Man prey'd not on his fellow-man, within

The hallow'd circle of his patriarch-sway,

That seem'd amidst barbarian clans around

A garden in a waste of brier and hemlock.

Ere life's meridian, thus that chief had reach'd,

The utmost pinnacle of savage grandeur,

And stood the envy of ignoble eyes,

The awe of humbler mortals, the example

Of youth's sublime ambition ; but to him,

It was not given to rest at any height ;

The thoughts that travel to eternity

Already had begun their pilgrimage,

Which time, nor change, nor life, nor death, could

   stop.

All that he saw, heard, felt, or could conceive,

Open'd new scenes of mental enterprise,

Imposed new tasks for arduous contemplation.

On the steep eminence which he had scaled

To rise or fall were sole alternatives ;

He might not stand, and he disdain'd to fall ;

Innate magnificence of mind upheld,

And buoyancy of genius bore him on.

Heaven, earth, and ocean, were to him familiar

In all their motions, aspects, changes ; each

To him paid tribute of the knowledge, hid

From unenquiring ignorance ; to him

Their gradual secrets, though with slow reserve,

Yet sure accumulation, all reveal'd.

But whence they came, even more than what they
were,

Awaken'd wonder, and defied conjecture ;

Blank wonder could not satisfy his soul,

And resolute conjecture would not yield,

Though foil'd a thousand times, in speculation

On themes that open'd immortality.

The gods whom his deluded countrymen

Acknowledged, were no gods to him ; he scorn'd

The impotence of skill that carved such figures,

And pitied the fatuity of those,

Who saw not in the abortions of their hands

The abortions of their minds. — 'Twas the Creator

He sought through every volume open to him,

From the small leaf that holds an insect's web,

From which ere long a colony shall issue

With wings and limbs as perfect as the eagle's,

To the stupendous ocean, that gives birth

And nourishment to everlasting millions

Of creatures, great and small, beyond the power

Of man to comprehend how they exist.

One thought amidst the multitude within him

Press'd with perpetual, with increasing weight,

And yet the elastic soul beneath its burthen

Wax'd strong and stronger, was enlarged, exalted,

With the necessity of bearing up

Against annihilation ; for that seem'd

The only refuge were this hope foregone :

It was as though he wrestled with an angel,

And would not let him go without a blessing,

If not extort the secret of his name :

This was that thought, that hope ; — dumb idols,

And the vain homage of their worshippers,

Were proofs to him, not less than sun and stars,

That there were beings mightier far than man,

Or man had never dream'd of aught above him :

'Twas clear to him as was his own existence,

In which he felt the fact personified,

That man himself was for this world too mighty,

Possessing powers which could not ripen here,

But ask'd infinity to bring them forth,

And find employ for their unbounded scope.

Tradition told him, that, in ancient time,

Sky, sun, and sea were all the universe ;

The sun grew tired of gazing on the sea,

Day after day ; then, with descending beams,

Day after day he pierced the dark abyss,

Till he had reach'd its diamantine floor ;

Whence he drew up an island, as a tree

Grows in the desert from some random seed,

Dropt by a wild bird. Grain by grain it rose,

And touch'd at length the surface ; there expanding

Beneath the fostering influence of his eye,

Prolific seasons, light, and showers, and dew,

Aided by earthquakes, hurricanes, volcanoes,

(All agents of the universal sun,)

Conspired to form, advance, enrich, and break

The level reef, till hills and dales appear'd,

And the small isle became a continent,

Whose bounds his ancestors had never traced.

Thither in time, by means inscrutable,

Plants, animals, and man himself were brought ;

And with the idolaters the gods they served.

These tales tradition told him ; he believed,

Though all were fables, yet they shadow'd truth ;

That truth with heart, soul, mind, and strength he
  sought.

O 'twas a spectacle for angels, bound

On embassies of mercy to this earth,

To gaze on with compassion and delight,

— Yea, with desire that they might be his helpers, —

To see a dark endungeon'd spirit roused,

And struggling into glorious liberty,

Though Satan's legions watch'd at every portal,

And held him by ten thousand manacles !

Such was the being whom I here descried,

And fix'd my earnest expectation on him ;

For now or never might my hope be proved,

How near, by searching, man might find out God.

Thus, while he walk'd along that peaceful valley,

Though rapt in meditation far above

The world which met his senses, but in vain

Would charm his spirit within its magic circle,

— Still with benign and meek simplicity

He hearken'd to the prattle of a babe,

Which he was leading by the hand ; but scarce

Could he restrain its eagerness to break

Loose, and run wild with joy among the bushes.

It was his grandson, now the only stay

Of his bereaved affections ; all his kin

Had fall'n before him, and his youngest daughter

Bequeath'd this infant with her dying lips :

" O take this child, my father ! take this child,

And bring it up for me ; so may it live

To be the latest blessing of thy life. "

He took the child ; he brought it up for her ;

It was the latest blessing of his life ;

And while his soul explored immensity,

In search of something undefinedly great,

This infant was the link which bound that soul

To this poor world, where he had not a wish

Or hope, beyond the moment, for himself.

The little one was dancing at his side,

And dragging him with petty violence

Hither and thither from the onward path,

To find a bird's nest or to hunt a fly :

His feign'd resistance and unfeign'd reluctance

But made the boy more resolute to rule

The grandsire with his fond caprice. The sage,

Though dallying with the minion's wayward will,

His own premeditated course pursued,

And while, in tones of sportive tenderness,

He answer'd all its questions, and ask'd others

As simple as its own, yet wisely framed

To wake and prove an infant's faculties ;

As though its mind were some sweet instrument,

And he, with breath and touch, were finding out

What stops or keys would yield the richest music :

— All this was by-play to the scene within

The busy theatre of his own breast.

Keen and absorbing thoughts were working there,

And his heart travail'd with unutter'd pangs ;

Sigh after sigh, escaping to his lips,

Was check'd, or turn'd into some lively word,

To hide the bitter conflict from his child.

At length they struck into the woods, and thence

Climb'd the grey rocks aloof. There from his crag,

At their abrupt approach, the startled eagle

Took wing above their heads ; the boy alarm'd,

— Nor less delighted when no peril came, —

Follow'd its flight with eyes and hands upraised,

And bounding forward on the verdant slope,

Watch'd it diminish, till a gnat, that cross'd

His sight, eclipsed it : when he look'd again

'Twas gone, and for an instant he felt sad,

Till some new object won his gay attention.

His grandsire stepp'd to take the eagle's stand,

And gaze at freedom on the boundless prospect,

But started back, and held his breath with awe,

So suddenly, so gloriously it broke

From heaven, earth, sea, and air, at once upon him.

The tranquil ocean roll'd beneath his feet ;

The shores on each hand lessen'd from the view ;

The landscape glow'd with tropical luxuriance ;

The sky was fleck'd with gold and crimson clouds,

That seem'd to emanate from nothing there,

Born in the blue and infinite expanse,

Where just before the eye might seek in vain

An evening shadow as a daylight star.

    There stood the patriarch amidst a scene

Of splendour and beatitude ; himself

A diadem of glory o'er the whole,

For none but he could comprehend the beauty,

The bliss diffused throughout the universe ;

Yet holier beauty, higher bliss he sought,

Of which that universe was but the veil,

Wrought with inexplicable hieroglyphics.

Here then he stood, alone but not forsaken

Of Him, without whose leave a sparrow falls not.

Wide open lay the Book of Deity,

The page was Providence : but none, alas !

Had taught him letters ; when he look'd, he wept

To feel himself forbidden to peruse it.

— " O for a messenger of mercy now,

Like Philip when he join'd the Eunuch's chariot !

O for the privilege to burst upon him,

And show the blind, the dead, the light of life ! "

I hush'd the exclamation, for he seem'd

To hear it ; turn'd his head, and look'd all round,

As if an eye invisible beheld him,

A voice had spoken out of solitude :

— Yea such an eye beheld him, such a voice

Had spoken ; but they were not mine ; his life

He would have yielded on the spot, to see

That eye ; to hear that voice, and understand it :

It was the eye of God, the voice of Nature.

All in a moment on his knees he fell ;

And with imploring arms, outstretch'd to heaven,

And eyes no longer wet with hopeless tears,

But beaming forth sublime intelligence ;

In words through which his heart's pulsation

    throbb'd,

And made mine tremble to their accents, — pray'd :

— " Oh ! if there be a Power above all power,

A Light above all light, a Name above

All other names, in heaven and earth ; that Power,

That Light, that Name I call upon. " – He paused,

Bow'd his hoar head with reverence, closed his eyes,

And with clasp'd hands upon his breast, began

In under-tones, that rose in fervency,

Like incense kindled on a holy altar,

Till his whole soul became one tongue of fire,

Of which these words were faint and poor expressions :

— " Oh ! if Thou art, Thou knowest that I am :

Behold me, hear me, pity me, despise not

The prayer, which – if Thou art – Thou hast inspired,

Or wherefore seek I now a God unknown ?

And feel for Thee, if haply I may find

In whom I live and move and have my being ?

Reveal Thyself to me ; reveal thy power,

Thy light, thy name, — that I may fear, adore,

Obey, — and oh ! that I might love Thee too !

For, if Thou art – it must be – Thou art good ;

And I would be the creature of thy goodness :

Oh ! hear and answer ; — let me know Thou hearest ;

— Know that as surely as Thou art, so surely

My prayer and supplication are accepted. "

He waited silently ; there came no answer :

The roaring of the tide beneath, the gale

Rustling the forest-leaves, the notes of birds,

And hum of insects, — these were all the sounds,

That met familiarly around his ear.

He look'd abroad ; there shone no light from heaven

But that of sunset ; and no shapes appear'd

But glistening clouds, which melted through the sky

As imperceptibly as they had come ;

While all terrestrial objects seem'd the same

As he had ever known them ; — still he look'd

And listen'd, till a cold sick feeling sunk

Into his heart, and blighted every hope.

Anon faint accents, from the sloping lawn

Beneath the crag where he was kneeling, rose,

Like supernatural echoes of his prayer :

— " A Name above all names, — I call upon. –

Thou art – Thou knowest that I am : — Reveal

Thyself to me ; — but, oh ! that I may love Thee !

For if Thou art, Thou must be good : — Oh ! hear,

And let me know Thou hearest ! " – Memory fail'd

The child ; for 'twas his grandchild, though he knew

    not,

— In the deep transport of his mind, he knew not

That voice, to him the sweetest of ten thousand,

And known the best, because the best beloved.

Again it cried : — " Thou art – Thou must be good :

    — Oh ! hear,

And let me know Thou hearest. " – Memory fail'd

The child, but feeling fail'd not ; tears of light

Slid down his cheek ; he too was on his knees,

Clasping his little hands upon his heart,

Unconscious why, yet doing what he saw

His grandsire do, and saying what he said.

For while he gather'd buds and flowers, to twine

A garland for the old grey hairs, whose locks

Were lovelier in his sight than all the blooms

On which the bees and butterflies were feasting,

The Patriarch's agony of spirit caught

His eye, his ear, his heart ; he dropt the flowers,

And kneeling down among them, wept and pray'd

Like him, with whom he felt such strange emotions

As rapt his infant-soul to heavenly heights ;

Though whence they sprang, and what they meant, he
   knew not ;

But they were good, and that was all to him,

Who wonder'd why it was so sweet to weep :

Nor would he quit his humble attitude,

Nor cease repeating fragments of that lesson,

Thus learnt spontaneously from lips, whose words

Were almost dearer to him than their kisses,

When on his lap the old man dandled him,

And told him simple stories of his mother.

Recovering thought, the venerable sire

Beheld, and recognized his darling boy,

Thus beautiful and innocent, engaged

In the same worship with himself. His heart

Leap'd at the sight ; he flung away despondence,

While joy unspeakable and full of glory

Broke through the pagan darkness of his soul.

He ran and snatch'd the infant in his arms,

Embraced him passionately, wept aloud,

And cried, scarce knowing what he said, — " My Son !

My Son ! there is a God ! there is a God ! "

" And, oh ! that I may love Thee too ! " rejoin'd

The child, whose tongue could find no other words

Than prayer ; — " for if Thou art, Thou must be

    good. "

— " He is ! He is ! and we will love Him too ;

Yea and be like Him, — good, for He is good ! "

Replied the ancient father in amazement.

Then wept they o'er each other, till the child
Exceeded, and the old man's heart reproved him
For lack of reverence in the excess of joy :
The ground itself seem'd holy ; heaven and earth
Full of the presence, felt not seen, of Him,
The Power above all power, the Light above
All light, the Name above all other names ;
Whom he had call'd upon, whom he had found,
Yet worshipp'd only as " the Unknown God, " —
That nearest step which uninstructed man
Can take, from Nature up to Deity.
To Him again, standing erect, he pray'd,
And while he pray'd, high in his arms he held
That dearest treasure of his heart, the child
Of his last dying daughter, — now the sole

Hope of his life, and orphan of his house.

He held him as an offering up to heaven,

A living sacrifice unto the God

Whom he invoked : — " Oh ! Thou who art ! " he cried.

" And hast reveal'd that mystery to me,

Hid from all generations of my fathers,

Or, if once known, forgotten and perverted ;

I may not live to learn Thee better here ;

But, oh ! let this my son, mine only son,

Whom thus I dedicate to Thee ; — let him,

Let him be taught thy will, and choose

Obedience to it ; — may he fear thy power,

Walk in thy light, now dawning out of darkness ;

And, oh ! my last, last prayer, — to him reveal

The unutterable secret of thy name ! "

He paused ; then with the transport of a seer

Went on : — " That Name may all my nation know ;

And all that hear it worship at the sound,

When Thou shalt with a voice from heaven proclaim

    it ;

And so it surely shall be. ”

                      “ For Thou art ;

And if Thou art, Thou must be good ! ” exclaim’d

The child, yet panting with the breath of prayer.

    They ceased ; then went rejoicing down the

        mountains,

Through the cool glen, where not a sound was heard,

Amidst the dark solemnity of eve,

But the loud purling of the little brook,

And the low murmur of the distant ocean.

Thence to their home beyond the hills in peace

They walk’d ; and when they reach’d their humble

    threshold,

The glittering firmament was full of stars.

— He died that night ; his grandchild lived to see

The Patriarch's prayer and prophecy fulfill'd.

Here ends my song ; here ended not the vision :

I heard seven thunders uttering their voices,

And wrote what they did utter ; but 'tis seal'd

Within the volume of my heart, where thoughts,

Unbodied yet in vocal words, await

The quickening warmth of poesy, to bring

Their forms to light, — like secret characters,

Invisible till open'd to the fire ;

Or like the potter's paintings, colourless

Till they have pass'd to glory through the flames.

Changes more wonderful than those gone by,

More beautiful, transporting, and sublime,

To all the frail affections of our nature,

To all the immortal faculties of man ;

Such changes did I witness ; not alone

In one poor Pelican Island, nor on one

Barbarian continent, where man himself

Could scarcely soar above the Pelican :

— The world as it hath been in ages past,

The world as now it is, the world to come,

Far as the eye of prophecy can pierce ; —

These I beheld, and still in memory's rolls

They have their pages and their pictures ; these,

Another day, a nobler song may show.

Vain boast ! another day may not be given ;

This song may be my last ; for I have reach'd

That slippery descent, whence man looks back

With melancholy joy on all he cherish'd ;

Around, with love unfeign'd, on all he's losing ;

Forward, with hope that trembles while it turns

To the dim point where all our knowledge ends.

I am but one among the living ; one

Among the dead I soon shall be ; and one

Among unnumber'd millions yet unborn ;

The sum of Adam's mortal progeny,

From Nature's birth-day to her dissolution :

— Lost in infinitude, my atom-life

Seems but a sparkle of the smallest star

Amidst the scintillations of ten thousand

Twinkling incessantly ; no ray returning

To shine a second moment, where it shone

Once, and no more for ever : — so I pass.

The world grows darker, lonelier, and more silent,

As I go down into the vale of years ;

For the grave's shadows lengthen in advance,

And the grave's loneliness appals my spirit,

And the grave's silence sinks into my heart,

Till I forget existence in the thought

Of non-existence, buried for a while

In the still sepulchre of my own mind,

Itself imperishable : — ah ! that word,

Like the archangel's trumpet, wakes me up

To deathless resurrection. Heaven and earth

Shall pass away, but that which thinks within me

Must think for ever ; that which feels must feel :

— I am, and I can never cease to be.

O thou that readest ! take this parable

Home to thy bosom ; think as I have thought,

And feel as I have felt, through all the changes,

Which Time, Life, Death, the world's great actors,

　　wrought,

While centuries swept like morning dreams before me,

And thou shalt find this moral to my song :

— Thou art, and thou canst never cease to be :

What then are time, life, death, the world to thee ?

I may not answer ; ask eternity.